Words in My Hands

A Teacher,
A Deaf-Blind Man,
An Unforgettable
Journey

DIANE CHAMBERS

To Mary,
a fellow writer
Best:
Diane Chambers

ELLEXA PRESS, LLC
Inspirational, Informative, and Entertaining Books

Ellexa Press, LLC, 32262 Steven Way, Conifer, CO 80433
dlc@ellexapress.CityMax.com

"Fugue" is printed with permission of Robert J. Smithdas.

ISBN   0-9760967-0-6
Library of Congress Control Number 2004096549

Cover photo by Stanley Grober
Cover and interior designed by F + P Graphic Design, Inc.

Contents

Acknowledgments

I would like to thank Bert Riedel and the Riedel family for giving me the extraordinary experience of being a part of their lives, and for giving me the green light to write this book.

Thanks to Becky Hawkins, past president of Foothills Writers group, and Marie Kriss, past president of the Denver chapter of the National League of American Pen Women, who believed in me and pushed me forward. Instructors Michael Henry and Lisa Turner and members of the Lighthouse Writers Workshop recognized value in my early writing and offered me suggestions and encouragement.

Thank you to editorial consultants Sandy Chapman, Suzanne Kita, and John Riedel, who worked with me through tough stages of the book. Thanks go to Joni Palen, my computer teacher, who guided me through frustrating times while I was both learning to use the computer and beginning to write this book. Thank you to Albert and Joanne Greenberg for their steadfast enthusiasm and support for my project.

I feel tremendous gratitude to those people who shared their recollections, without which I could not have undertaken this project: Shana Atlee, Ann Cobb, Jean Dent, Andrea Duyckers, Vera Feistel, Barbara Galoob, Peggy Grant, Alfredia Harris, Eloise Heller, Jean Kelly, Rich Lamb, Marian Lidicker, Rita May, Kate Moulton, Blake and Ali

Porch, Janet Ray, John and Mary Riedel, Iola and Durl Rohr, Carrie Sigman, Marie Van den Bosch, and Amy, Jake, Marcia, and Tim Vastine.

Thanks to attorneys Mitch Anstedt and Richard Arnold for their legal insights on the deaf; and to those who gave assistance with information and research: Lindsey Antle, interpreter trainer; Laverne Dell, blind consultant of the Vocational Rehabilitation Center in Denver; Leilani J. Johnson, director of Distance Opportunities for Interpreter Training Center; Sue Ann Von Feldt, certified interpreter and former employee of the Colorado School for the Deaf and Blind; David Farrell, principal of the Colorado School for the Deaf and Blind; Alvin Roberts, quality assurance administrator, Bureau of Blind Services, Carbondale, Illinois; Linda Roberts, reference librarian of the Helen M. Plum Memorial Library; Michele Renusch and Christine Visser, members of the Deaf community; and Bruse Visser, deaf-blind consumer and consultant.

I owe many hugs to Jody Berman, my editor, who helped me through every revision and every stage of this book's production. Credit also goes to the book's designer, Rebecca Finkel.

Mostly, I am indebted to my children who believed in me and understood while I toiled so many hours away from them, and to my husband who lent incredible patience while I learned and grew through this endeavor.

Author's Note

With all due respect to family members and to various opinions regarding how events took place in this book, I have re-created them to the best of my ability from Bert's and my perspectives. For purposes of confidentiality and privacy, some names and identifying information have been changed. Where real names have been used, it has been with the individuals' permission.

Prologue

en minutes before meeting my new sign language student, eighty-six-year-old Bert Riedel, I knew I was in for something unlike anything I'd experienced before. Walking into the Riedel home for the first time, I heard Bert, a deaf-blind man, playing Beethoven on the piano. In my more than twenty years of working as a sign language interpreter, the silence of deafness had usually shut people out from the music that hearing people enjoy, and from communication that hearing people take for granted. If a deaf person were also blind, they were shut out even more.

When I came into Bert's deaf-blind world, I brought with me all I had learned about deafness, mostly through my work as an interpreter. I had begun my training at the age of twenty-two, when I thought interpreting simply meant listening to the speaker and putting signs onto their words. It wasn't long until I became aware that interpreting was much more complicated than that, as I became immersed in what not being able to hear means. When I wasn't in the depths of interpreting, I was a teacher, an advocate, a counselor, or a friend.

My appreciation of how profound the effects of deafness can be came initially when I met eighteen-year-old Jason. He had been deprived of language and education until age eight, at which time he started learning sign language from his adoptive parents. At eighteen, Jason, who rode a one-speed bicycle to get around, had the normal teenage aspiration to drive a car. Yet with only a third-grade reading level, he was unable to read the driver's education manual. I was hired to teach him this information along with some basic math. I signed and drew pictures to teach him.

Jason often got into skirmishes when he misperceived situations with people who didn't understand his limitations. One day he described to me, through signs and gestures, how a truck nearly collided with him and that the driver tried to run him over. Jason said he reported the misdeed to a police officer, who then went off to track down the truck.

Knowing Jason couldn't have spoken to the officer, I asked him, through sign, "How did you talk to the policeman?" He pulled a crumpled note out of his pocket. On it he had written, "*Do did truck brown.*" I suspected the policeman had no idea what to make of the note, nor did he do anything about the brown truck. Because Jason hadn't learned enough language during his formative years, he wasn't able to comprehend that the policeman could not possibly know what he knew about the brown truck.[1]

Under my tutelage, Jason mastered subtraction that summer. We had only scratched the surface in the driver's education manual and were just moving onto division when the tutoring funds ran out. For a long time after that I wondered whether anyone ever taught Jason division, and I remained concerned about his future.

With the language barrier of deafness comes a cultural gap between the deaf and the hearing. Bridging the gap can be challenging and complex. In the legal system, for example, I've seen city attorneys drop cases against developmentally deaf defendants for minor offenses rather than proceed with measures like psychological testing to determine the defendant's competency to stand trial. Doing so would be too cumbersome and expensive. One reason is that there are inherent problems in translating psychological tests into the language and culture of the deaf. Psychologists ask questions like, "What does 'Strike while the iron is hot' mean to you?" or "What does "People who live in glass houses should not throw stones' mean?" or "Do you hear voices?" These language concepts are foreign to the deaf mind. I've had to inform psychologists before they administer the tests that deaf people are not familiar with English proverbs and idioms and that sometimes deaf people *can* hear people's voices if they are a certain pitch.

If a deaf person answers *yes* to hearing voices, it is important to understand the difference between one who is experiencing auditory hallucinations and one who is simply hearing garbled speech.

The most severe consequences of deafness that I've seen have involved deaf minorities from rural areas who had poor access to formal education. One deaf juvenile came to the United States from an impoverished country and was placed in various foster homes before being placed with a family who communicated in American Sign Language. From them he learned some sign language and began his schooling, but it was too late for him to garner the morals and ethics he needed to conform to society's rules. Legal troubles ensued in his teen years when he began to display deviant bathroom behaviors and engage in petty crimes. I was called to interpret between him and his social workers, teachers, and a judge. The issues were clouded by whether his lack of morals and ethics were due to his language dearth, psychological problems, a learning disability, mental illness, or a combination of these.

His deafness and the language barrier were at the forefront of every issue, leaving the professionals scratching their heads as they ran out of options on where to place this ward of the state. The professionals couldn't decide whether he belonged in a hospital, a school, a prison, a family of his ethnic background, or simply a family that could sign.

Certainly not all of my work bridging the gap between the hearing and the deaf has involved troubling cases — those are at the extreme end. Over the years, in numerous types of settings, I've met hundreds of deaf people of varying intellectual skills and abilities — many of them fine and brilliant human beings. Each of them who live in the silent world have taught me something about broken ears.

My decision to write this book was inspired by what I learned from them, but especially from Bert Riedel. Despite the gradual loss of his hearing and his sight in his youth, Bert became a musician and a dentist. Later, totally deaf and blind at eighty-six years old, he continued to persevere and became my sign language student. Hired by Bert's son and daughter-in-law, whom he lived with, my job was to teach them signs so they could communicate more easily. Bert and I continued to work together for five years. With forty-two years between us, Bert had a lot to teach me as well. What ensued was life-changing for us both. *Words in My Hands* is our story.

CHAPTER ONE

He's Eighty-six?

I trudged through the construction equipment in our garage and into the house, lugging books, mail, and my lunch cooler with its stale remains. The door slammed behind me as I dropped my armload onto the newspapers scattered across the kitchen table. It was late March 1998 and I was tired and hungry from a long day of interpreting. Jim, my husband, and Matthew, my seventeen-year-old son, stood in the kitchen, looking at me as if they were asking, "What's for dinner?" With our nineteen-year-old daughter, Heather, away at college, it was only the three of us.

Dirty dishes cluttered the counter, left over from our hurried breakfasts. The phone was ringing. I felt stressed and started toward the phone, then decided to let Matthew answer it — the phone was for him most of the time anyway. I gathered the newspapers from the table instead.

"Hello," Matt said, in his low monotone. As he stepped toward me, I dropped the newspapers into the trash. He handed me the phone. "Mom, it's for you."

It was Mary Riedel calling. "We understand you teach sign language," she said. "We got your name from Barb Coffan."

"Yes, I've known her for many years," I said. Barb was an expert in deaf-blind interpreting.

"My father-in-law is eighty-six," Mary continued. "He's deaf and blind and lives with us. We wanted to know if you'd be interested in teaching us some basic signs."

Eighty-six-years old, I thought, and he wants to learn sign language? Learning a second language is difficult and becomes more so the older one gets. During my twenty-one years in the field of sign language interpretation, I'd encountered many people who said they wanted to learn sign language, and then they never pursued it. Others said they knew sign language but actually knew only a handful of signs. Many people do achieve a level of sign communication, but few master the language unless they're children of deaf parents or they study to become interpreters.

"He's eighty-six, you say?"

"Yes. His name's Bert. He swims and lifts weights. He's very active. We just want to learn some basic signs," she repeated.

"Does he have Usher Syndrome?"

"Yes . . . so, you're familiar with that?"

"I am. I see a fair amount of people with Usher Syndrome. I'm very comfortable with deaf-blindness."

We spoke a bit more. I wanted to assess the situation before I made a commitment.

Usher Syndrome is a genetic disorder that affects approximately thirty thousand to forty thousand people in the United States. It causes a hearing impairment, coupled with the degeneration of the retinas of the eyes.[2] Some families have more than one member with the syndrome. I find it interesting that most people have never heard of Usher Syndrome. In one case, I knew a family who had two deaf siblings, both in their thirties, who were losing their sight. They didn't know about the syndrome that was causing their problem. One of the siblings knew sign language. The other didn't and was doing nothing to prepare for the huge communication obstacles that would inevitably occur.

While the syndrome is always characterized by the loss of these two senses, there are three variations, categorized according to the time of onset of the blindness or deafness. The fifty or so people I know with Usher Syndrome are all Type I and II. They were born deaf or hard of hearing and communicate in sign language; their blindness came later in their lives.

Only three to six percent of all deaf people have Usher Syndrome, but I can easily spot those who are in the process of losing their vision by the way they walk. They're usually a little off-balance and often bump into things unnoticed in their periphery. Because of their decreased side vision, they sometimes pull back in surprise when something comes into their line of sight, or they need to step backward, putting more distance between us to get all my signs into their boundary of sight. Some of these people aren't even aware that their vision isn't normal, but the ones who are tell me it helps if we move into better light so they can see my signs better. Sometimes, I need to repeat signs they missed or keep my signing space confined to a smaller area.

Since the Riedels were just now wanting to learn sign language at Bert's late age, I assumed Bert had Usher Syndrome Type III, meaning he was already blind before his deafness came.

I loved teaching sign language and enjoyed interpreting for the deaf-blind. Mary Riedel's request was not for interpreting, however, and I'd never done the kind of teaching she was wanting. Furthermore, Bert was elderly. Ever since childhood, I'd never had much of a comfort level with older people. They scared me. I remember our old, unkempt neighbor, Mr. Mac, who used to snap my fingers and my best friend Cindy's beneath the rubber bands wrapped around the arm of his rocking chair. With his trembling hand, Mr. Mac would stretch the rubber bands up from the wooden arm. "Put your fingers under there," he'd say. We fell for it every time. He'd let go of the rubber bands, and if we weren't fast enough to pull our tiny fingers away before the bands snapped tight, we were caught with a sting, and he would laugh, showing a mouthful of stained and missing teeth.

But now, Mary did have me interested. Although her father-in-law was elderly, I felt sure there would be no rubber bands to contend with. "Where did you say you live?"

"Conifer, but we're willing to go anywhere."

I lived in Conifer, too. A mountain community. This would be a rare opportunity for me to work close to home. Most of my other assignments were at least an hour's commute into Denver. It would probably only amount to a few lessons anyway.

"I'm very busy, but . . . sure," I said. "I'd like to do that. How about at the end of the week?"

We agreed on Friday.

You Interpreter?

A long with my work as an interpreter, I'd held various other positions over the years in my field. One was a summer job in Denver's Capitol Hill neighborhood, teaching swimming to deaf children in 1978. By the next summer, while pregnant with my first child, Heather, I had transformed the swimming classes into a summer day camp for kids in that same neighborhood, with some deaf and some physically disabled kids mixed in. For thirteen summers I wore numerous hats while performing that job — director, teacher, interpreter, swimming instructor, and mother to my own two children who came to work with me.

I had a lot of ambition, energy, and patience during those years. But by the time Heather reached twelve and Matthew ten, the responsibilities of running the summer program were taking a toll on me as my family was being pulled in the direction of gymnastics for my daughter and soccer for my son. My family was outgrowing the day camp experience and ready for a change, so I resigned.

Right away, I began interpreting full time in a variety of community settings, working mostly with adults. I missed the kids, but I loved interpreting. I met hundreds of people and thrived on the interesting variety of assignments and the flexibility my job afforded. I drove somewhere different every day, and there were always new challenges.

Soon I was about to embark on yet another new challenge, but I had one more day until I'd meet Bert.

It was Thursday, and I had two interpreting assignments. Just as I had done many times before, I walked into a doctor's office waiting room and scanned the room for a deaf woman I hadn't met. Most of the people in the room were seated, looking down at magazine articles. Hearing people don't have to look up to know what's transpiring around them. They use their ears to tell them. Deaf people are usually watching everything that's going on. I made eye contact with the only one who was looking up.

"You deaf?" I signed.

She signed back. "Yes, you interpreter?"

"Yes, how know?"

"Your book. Interpreter always have book." She was referring to my assignment book. She was right about that. I always had it with me. We both nodded, smiling.

I took a seat across from her. "My name D-i-a-n-e," I fingerspelled.

"Nice, meet you, my name W-e-n-d-y."

We nodded again. The head nodding was customary in sign language, in acknowledging one another. "Not meet you before," I signed.

"No, not meet you, same. Where from?" she signed, without mouthing the words.

I followed suit with her signing style. "I born here, grow up here. Where school you?"

"C-S-D-B. Before live small town," and she spelled the name of a farming town.

"Then third grade back forth C-S-D-B. Parents hearing, two brother, one sister, all hearing. Me one deaf." There was more smiling and head nodding between us. "How learn sign? Parents deaf?" she asked. Deaf people are always curious as to where or why hearing people learn sign language.

"No, my parents not deaf. I learn sign twenty-three years ago, summer job in Lakewood, some deaf kids there." Not only was it where I began learning sign, but the experience would inspire the day camp I'd create three years later.

I glanced aside and noticed the nurse standing at the doorway. "Wendy?" she called out.

Wendy watched me point to the nurse and then to her. We followed the nurse into one of examination rooms.

Our waiting room conversation told me many things I didn't have to ask Wendy about—things that helped me communicate with her. I gathered she was a deaf child born into a hearing family that probably didn't know sign language and was ill equipped to deal with the implications of deafness. She had attended the deaf residential school, Colorado School for the Deaf and Blind in Colorado Springs, where she stayed during the week, returning home by bus on weekends.

At the deaf school, American Sign Language (ASL) is used, which is a natural language among the deaf. Its gestures, body language, and facial expressions develop inherently when a person has no hearing. ASL has its own grammar and idioms and is distinct from Signed English, where the words are mouthed while being signed in English word order. The benefit of attending a state residential school for the deaf is full-time interaction with people who use the same language. This means that students become adept at social communication. However, it is often true that their academic stimulation is not on par with hearing students in regular education. Additionally, when deaf students are separated from their hearing families, they seldom develop fluent communication with their family members. They come to the residential school lacking the incidental learning that normally takes place in family conversation. Because busy teachers can't make up for this language and informational dearth, it's not unusual for many of these students to achieve only a fourth- to fifth-grade reading level by graduation. Although this statistic has remained unchanged for fifty years,[3] trends are now showing that early language intervention for deaf babies under six months of age can result in nearly normal development.[4]

Nevertheless, it's difficult to acquire English skills without hearing the language. Many deaf five-year-olds barely know one thousand words as compared with hearing kindergarteners who already have a vocabulary of five thousand to six thousand words.[5] Without this early language, a person's cognitive, social, and literacy skills are all affected. Many people aren't aware of this problem in deafness; consequently, a huge gap of understanding is often left between deaf and hearing people.

My job as an interpreter was to bridge this gap to the best of my ability. But sometimes I felt I was the only one in the room cognizant of how large the gap really was. However, as conversation flowed smoothly between Wendy and her doctor, I knew I had successfully done my job.

It was thirty miles to my next assignment, the courtroom where I was to team up with a relay interpreter—a deaf person trained in interpreting. A deputy was the only one in the courtroom when I arrived. "Hello, I'm the sign language interpreter for Eduardo Ramos," I told him.

"Uh, he's in custody," he said. "We'll be bringin' him up in a minute. Yeah, he uses that sign language. How do you do that with the Spanish?" he asked.

"I use American Sign Language," I said. "It's not Spanish."

"Oh, this guy uses Spanish."

"Really?" I said, suspecting this was not the case. I'd been in situations before where Hispanic deaf people communicated in ASL while their families spoke only Spanish. They needed me as well as a Spanish interpreter just so the family members could talk to each other.

"I'm expecting a team interpreter who will be working with me," I said. "If we could talk to the defendant for a few minutes before we get started, we can assess whether or not we can communicate with him."

Working with relay interpreters always requires an explanation to people—hearing people especially. It is hard for them to grasp that the high-level legalese used in the courtroom isn't easily translated into a signed language readily understood by most deaf people. Sign language is my second language. I learned it late in life. It is the relay interpreter's first language. A relay has deafness, language, and a cultural heritage in common with a deaf defendant. A relay interpreter understands better than I how a deaf person thinks.

Trained and certified to work in these legal settings, the relay is able to follow and comprehend a hearing interpreter's formal courtroom signing. The relay conveys the same information to a deaf client in a signed language more unique to the "Deaf culture," whose members identify themselves by a capital *D* in the word *Deaf*. The idea behind using relay interpreting teams is to eliminate potential linguistic and cultural misunderstandings.

When my team interpreter arrived, we read over the case file together before the judge came in. Then we met Mr. Ramos. We determined he did indeed use ASL and not spoken Spanish or Spanish Sign Language. We wouldn't have been able to proceed otherwise.

"All rise!" the bailiff's voice rang out. "The court is now in session. The honorable Judge Marquist presides." The judge entered from the door to the right of the bench and took his seat. "You may be seated," he said. He called our case first. I interpreted to my deaf relay. He signed to Mr. Ramos as we began interpreting the proceedings.

"We are here today to advise you of your rights and the charges against you, Mr. Ramos." I stood slightly behind Mr. Ramos at the lectern and signed the judge's words as they were spoken. The relay focused on me as he stood near the judge's bench and transformed my signed legalese into visual concepts for the defendant. As the judge continued, I held his words in my mind while I watched the progress of my team interpreter. The challenge for me was always listening to the new information as it was being spoken and storing it while I monitored what the relay was doing—and then signing it when the relay looked back to me, ready to receive it.

"You are charged with assault, and battery . . . which allegedly occurred on February 18th at approximately 4:30 p.m. at the residence of— "

As interpreters are sometimes humorously referred to as "interrupters," after I signed the judge's statement, I politely interrupted him. "Your Honor, may the interpreters have just a moment to convey that information?"

"Certainly." He waited for a moment and mumbled something to the attorneys.

I could tell they were uncomfortable with the disruption to their normal routine, but they respectfully waited for us to do our work.

"Police say you light, grab, cord pull, throw, hurt face," the relay interpreter signed. Already familiar with the situation from the police report, the relay mimed grabbing the lamp and yanking its cord out from the wall before throwing it across the room and then showed someone getting hit in the face. "Happen, February 18, time 4:30 afternoon."

The relay interpreter finished signing the charges to Mr. Ramos and looked back at me to continue. The judge proceeded to speak and we resumed the process until we were dismissed. With my highly skilled teammate, the process was amazing. Our two brains and four hands had transformed the judge's words into a language more closely matching that of the deaf defendant's. In the reverse, we had successfully communicated the deaf man's response back to the judge.

There's a big difference in interpreting for someone deaf who was born to deaf parents rather than to hearing parents, as were my clients, Wendy and Mr. Ramos. In families where everyone is deaf, the babies have access to language early and usually develop on a normal schedule because there's no lag time in acquiring language. When the child grows up, he or she is typically fluent in both ASL and English and has more high-level reading and communication skills. This deaf adult typically understands more English-type signing, whereas Mr. Ramos did not. From a lack of early exposure to language, he had developed only minimal communication skills.

When blindness is coupled with deafness, interpreting is even more intricate. It requires tactile signing. I sign directly into the hands of the blind person, allowing him or her to feel the shapes and movements. This kind of interpreting involves continuous physical contact and may require slower signing if the topic is something new. Adding emotional and environmental information to the interpretation is crucial for a deaf-blind person to know what's going on in the room. For instance, I might sign,

"The doctor and nurse are here. The doctor is smiling. The doctor is a woman and she wants to know if you . . ." And later, "The doctor is gone. We are waiting. She will bring your chart." When the doctor returns I sign, "The doctor is here now. Doctor is upset. She can't find your chart."

Many interpreters have little training in this arena or are uncomfortable with the adaptations involved. To where they shy away, I am lured.

And so I was drawn to meet Bert.

• • • • •

On Friday, I walked up the steps to the Riedels' front door. Although the house looked new and was well kept, I wondered what kind of home or family life would await me inside. I'd been to people's homes on assignments before—usually accompanying a social worker—and I had encountered a myriad of living environments. Some assignments were in old apartment buildings where the halls reeked of cigarette smoke. Others were in subsidized housing that smelled from old and stained carpet. The living quarters in those places were small, and sometimes deaf friends of the tenant's were also there, coming and going while I interpreted. I had sat on torn furniture, and there were times when a deaf mother's small child had crawled lovingly into my lap as I signed.

There were no distinctive odors or children running about as I rang the Riedels' doorbell and waited on the stoop. What awakened my senses was music coming from a piano. Too many years had passed since my music appreciation class in college. I couldn't recognize the composer, but Mozart came to mind. Then a woman with dark curly hair and a warm smile opened the door. "Are you Diane?" she asked.

"Yes, you must be Mary."

She invited me in and I followed her past the living room into the kitchen. I don't know how I knew it, but something told me it was Bert playing the piano. "Is that *him* playing?" I asked, referring to the beautiful sounds streaming from the adjoining room. My heart skipped a couple of beats at the thought of a deaf person playing music like that. A tingle rushed through my body, raising the hair on my arms. My throat tightened. I tried to hide the tears filling my eyes when she answered *yes*.

He continued to play in the background as I tried to compose myself. Mary was showing me the electronic brailler, the machine they used to communicate with Bert. It consisted of a laptop computer connected by a cable to the brailler—a black box, about the same size as the laptop. When they typed what they wanted to say onto the laptop, the words were relayed to the brailler. A strip of tiny pegs then popped up through pin-size holes, making the braille dots that corresponded with the typist's words. Bert read the dots with his index finger. I'd never seen a machine like this—a PowerBraille Display. They called it the power brailler.

Because of his Usher Syndrome, Bert had become deaf and blind in his later years, and had learned to read braille. Now the machine was their only means of communication. Although Bert was born with near normal hearing and vision, he was left legally blind by age forty-two. His deafness followed and gradually became profound.

Bert finished playing the piece, which I later learned was Beethoven's "Pathetique."

"I'll get him now," Mary said. "He's expecting you."

I felt nervous. How do you meet a stranger who is both deaf and blind? I was experienced in using tactile communication with other deaf-blind people, but Bert didn't use this form of communication. He didn't know any sign language. I waited at the kitchen table with the machine for a few moments until Bert and Mary appeared.

He walked with short steps behind Mary, holding onto the crook of her arm with one hand, extending his white cane with the other. I was struck first by his clean, fluffy white hair. He wore a freshly laundered plaid flannel shirt and neat corduroy pants. When they came near enough Mary stepped aside. I reached out and took Bert's free hand in mine, and then instinctively I hugged him.

"Hellooo. How *are* you?" he said. There was music and vitality in his voice and a sparkle in his smile. In a wink of time with no words from me, we had connected and I knew this was going to be something good.

No Plan, No Method

I came to the Riedels' house with the notion that three or four sessions would suffice to teach the family some basic signs. Beyond that, I had no idea what to expect from them. I had asked Mary to have a list ready with words they thought would be most useful. I expected the list to include simple words like *bathroom, eat, drink,* and *shoes.* It took me by surprise to see that the list began with *errands, exercise,* and *neighbors.*

I could see at once this family was active, but when Mary mentioned that Bert used to be a dentist, I also realized he was educated and that they all were most likely serious about learning. Simple words were not going to be enough for them. There was no sign for *errands* in ASL. One had to construct it using other signs, which was far more advanced than what I had anticipated for our first lesson. I threw out my original plan. I would improvise.

Then I met John. He came into the kitchen and introduced himself. He was considerably taller than his father but had the same blue eyes and was every bit as warm and friendly. There was something else about him, too. Something more subtle. It had to do with his keenness for what we were about to do.

After the introductions, I suggested a seating arrangement around the small kitchen table where the list and the power brailler rested. I sat next to Bert. Without any

experience on the machine—I didn't know how to incorporate it with what I had planned to do—I started doing
what I knew best. I positioned myself face to face with Bert,
with one knee between his. It was more comfortable for
our backs this way, so that when I took his hands in mine,
one of us didn't have to sit twisted. I appointed John as the
interpreter for the day.
He would translate my
spoken words to Bert via
the power brailler, leaving
my hands free to demon-
strate the language the
three of them wanted to
learn.

I was too nervous to
think about breaking the
ice by telling them some-
thing about myself or
even giving an introduc-
tion to sign language. I

Photo reprinted with permission from Eliot Khuner Photography.

John and Mary Riedel.

just started teaching. "We use our index finger to point to
each other to mean *you* and *me*, *he* and *she*," I began. With
my hands in my lap, I waited while John typed and Bert
read the braille aloud. He spoke clearly, with no loss of
quality in his voice from age or his deafness.

Then I took Bert's hands and he kept them on mine
as I demonstrated the sign. I touched my chest with my
right index finger. "Me," I said. I touched Bert's chest with
the same finger: "You." I pointed to his left to indicate
where Mary was sitting. "She." Bert's blue eyes gazed out
into darkness, but behind them, he followed along intently,
going back and forth from my hands to the brailler. We listened as Bert translated the brailled words.

Because Bert was responsible for feeding Rocky, the Riedels' dog, I taught the signs for *dog* and *hungry.* Combining these signs could make four sentences: *You hungry. Me hungry. She hungry. Dog hungry.* Next we tackled the letters *B, J,* and *M,* from which we could make up a name sign for each person in the family.

"This is the letter *B.*" I held my hand with the palm facing out, the fingers upright, and my thumb folded against my palm. John and Mary copied my hand shape and accepted it without question. Bert did not. With a puzzled expression, he studied my hand shape carefully, feeling it with both of his hands. "Why is this a letter *B*?" he asked.

I knew the sign language seemed obscure to him, but in time it would become second nature, just like a child learning how to read. He would have to trust me.

"That's just the hand shape that was created for that letter," I answered. "Then we can use it to give you a name sign. When we tap our shoulder with the letter *B*, it will mean Bert." As I taught, John was managing three different roles as student, interpreter, and typist. Bert continued going from me to the brailler.

"What's a name sign?" Bert asked.

"It's a symbol to represent that person." I showed them my name sign, which is composed of the letter *D.* I pointed my index finger straight up with the tip of my thumb touching the tips of the remaining curled-down fingers. The hand shape looks just like a small letter *d.* Starting at the top of my head, I moved my letter *d* down alongside my face to my chest in a gesture to represent my long hair. "The long hair I used to have," I told them.

"Now the letter *M.*" I knew Bert was still puzzled, yet he didn't appear frustrated—just interested in figuring out this new game. We continued, with my giving John and

Mary each name signs, too. I explained the signs, showed Bert how to configure them on his hands, and then let him feel the signs on my hands, so he could learn to interpret them. That was the ultimate goal. I hoped I wasn't overwhelming him.

John explained to me that they used one tap on Bert's arm to mean *no* and two taps to mean *yes.* I raised my eyebrows when I heard that. There are formalized signs for *yes* and *no,* and that tapping seemed barbaric to me. My impulse was to change their tapping code, but that could wait until another day.

After an hour we were left exhausted yet energized. At this point, I doubted Bert had any clue about what sign language could do for him. Still, he seemed to have enjoyed the interaction. Like teacher Anne Sullivan when she first met Helen Keller, who was blind and deaf since the age of nineteen months, I saw the potential here. This family was motivated. Bert's mind was sharp and he showed interest in learning. I knew this would take a lot of work, but I believed we could do it.

As I left that day and for the next week, I couldn't dismiss thoughts about Anne Sullivan. Although she was much younger than I, not quite twenty-one when she began teaching Helen, I sensed there were some similarities between us. Months later, when I read more about her, I learned that when she arrived at the Kellers' home in 1887, it was in March, the same month in which I arrived at the Riedels'. Like me, she brought no formal training in teaching the deaf-blind. Her only experience was that she herself was visually impaired and had lived for six years in the same cottage with Laura Bridgman, a deaf-blind woman, at the Perkins Institute for the Blind. Laura was the first deaf-blind person to be educated at the institute.

Before Helen Keller, she was the first to learn how to communicate by fingerspelling and how to read and to write. Where most of the blind students moved on after graduation, Laura lived nearly her entire life at the institute.[6]

Anne Sullivan came to the Kellers' with no plan or method, bringing only her knowledge of Laura Bridgman and her own intuition. Anne wrote to Sophia Hopkins, a friend and matron at the Perkins Institute, after only a couple of months into her pedagogy with Helen: "I know that she has remarkable powers and I believe that I shall be able to develop and mould them. I cannot tell how I know these things. I had no idea a short time ago how to go to work; I was feeling about in the dark."[7]

Similarly, I came with no plan or method from which to teach Bert—only my experience and intuition. And I shared Anne Sullivan's "fearless willingness to experiment."[8] Granted, my pupil, unlike Helen Keller, already had language, but he was eighty-six years old. He did not have the pliable brain of a child or a fascination with all things new. Could he learn a new language? We would see.

I could hardly wait for our next lesson the following week. I wanted to know what the Riedels had thought about our first meeting. Like a kid, I counted the days until Friday came around again.

• • • • •

"So, how was your week?" I asked Mary, as she led me into her kitchen for our second lesson.

"You saved my life," she said smiling.

My eyes opened wide with curiosity. "What happened?"

"I took him with me to town to do some errands. In the car driving from place to place, he never stopped talking. He asked me one question after another all day. I couldn't answer even one of them or tell him where we were. I was going crazy."

Mary went on to explain that at their last stop, she pulled into a restaurant parking lot, frazzled and drained from listening to Bert and leading him in and out of buildings. Suddenly, like magic, two of the signs they had learned that first day came to her mind: *you-hungry*. She signed them into his hands.

A light of understanding went on in Bert's head. "Are we at McDonalds?"

Mary tapped him twice. "Yes," she yelled triumphantly into the air. "It worked!"

Like a Light Bulb

In the next several lessons with the Riedels, we worked on a list of words for beginners, including the signs for *yes* and *no*. John and Mary learned a new sign within a minute because they could see. For Bert, it took a lot longer. His style of learning was totally different. Bert liked to ask questions and study the feel of the signs. He liked to ponder their significance and design his own mental associations to inscribe them into his memory.

Nevertheless, the four of us were having fun learning and laughing. Fairly soon, however, it became apparent that Bert was falling behind and getting left out of the amusement the rest of us were enjoying. I found myself pulled apart by two separate challenges. Bert needed my sole attention and I wanted to give it to him. At the same time, I wanted to focus on John and Mary. I knew they could sail through these beginning lessons, but they were being held back by Bert's slower pace. If I tried to proceed more quickly for them, Bert would get lost. If I slowed down for Bert, Mary would start taking phone calls at the table or work on paying her bills. It was frustrating me, but who could blame her for getting bored with our slow progress? In this group situation, I was struggling to do justice to everyone's individual needs and preserve my own sanity. Part of my struggle was that I was aware, but didn't believe the Riedels were, of how difficult it can be for adults to

Bert and I work on a sign language lesson at the kitchen table.

learn sign language. Learning individual signs is easy; construction of the entire language is very complex. From personal experience, I knew it could take years to become proficient.

Before 1975, I'd never seen sign language. It had been, more or less, a hidden language. Historically, many hearing people considered sign language primitive and even obscene because it used the body and facial expressions in a manner considered unbecoming. For a hundred years, most schools forbade its use because they believed if deaf children depended on sign language, they wouldn't learn to speak or lip-read English. There were stories of children who, if caught signing at school or on the playground, "had their hands struck with a ruler, or even bound together in an effort to force them to use their voices."[9]

Attitudes started to change in the 1960s when researchers discerned that American Sign Language did indeed possess all of the elements of a true language and wasn't simply crude gestures. From this awareness, a philosophy of "Total Communication" emerged in the 1970s. It included a method of signing that combined spoken words with signs, referred to as Simultaneous Communication, or what some called Signed English. It is distinct from ASL, which cannot be combined with spoken English because ASL has its own structure and grammar that do not conform to English word order.

Educators rapidly began adopting the Total Communication philosophy, and schools were employing the Simultaneous Communication method or variations of it. This is the method I was first exposed to. After college I worked at a summer camp for disabled children, including some deaf. A few of the staff used sign language as they spoke to the deaf children. Since it was the first time I'd seen it, I couldn't understand the children's signs nor could I understand their speech when they tried to communicate with me. Every day, I found myself longing to know what they were saying.

Consequently, I took a sign language class that fall and immediately became enamored with the language. Where for years I had dreamed of being a physical therapist, suddenly I had new goals. I started taking more sign language classes, and while working as a reading teacher's aide with hearing first- and second-graders, I pursued opportunities where I could use this new skill.

My first job in the field was as a tutor/interpreter at a junior high school. The administrator who hired me was a former teacher of the deaf and a proponent of the oral method. She didn't know sign language. That was in 1977, two years after Congress passed Public Law 94-142, the Education for All Handicapped Children Act (now called Individuals with Disabilities Education Act, or IDEA). The law provided all disabled students with the option to be educated in the "least restrictive environment." As a result, hearing-impaired children began to be mainstreamed into public schools with auxiliary services. Many were placed into regular classrooms and needed the assistance of interpreters. As large numbers of deaf students were no longer being sent to state residential schools, public school administrators were scrambling to hire tutor/interpreters in order to comply with the new law. Partly out of desperation, but mostly from a lack of knowledge of the intricacies involved in educating deaf children, they set about hiring anyone who could wave their hands in the air.

I was one of those people. At twenty-four, with only one year of sign language study, I believed I knew the language. That, along with my one year of teacher's aide experience, was apparently enough to convince the woman who hired me that I was qualified, and she placed me at a school with five deaf students. I was teamed with a deaf teacher my same age. Like me, she had learned sign language late because she wasn't born deaf. However, she began learning earlier than I, during college, as she was gradually losing her hearing. With her, I soon realized that my one year of sign language classes had been grossly inadequate and that I knew a lot less than I thought I did. Even so, the teacher graciously accepted me into her classroom. That's when my sign language training really began.[10]

In 1980 when my daughter, Heather, was born, I quit working for the school system but kept my hand in the profession by doing community interpreting part time. Working with adults, my fluency in ASL advanced and my interpreting ability matured. In 1984 I passed the national examination and became certified by the Registry of Interpreters for the Deaf. Reaching this milestone was an achievement, but it didn't mean my learning was complete. Mastering sign language was a lifelong process. I recognized the work that lay ahead for the Riedels, if they chose to pursue it.

• • • • •

As I tried to hold onto my sanity during the early lessons with the Riedels, I imagined that Anne Sullivan may have felt the same way when she first began working with Helen Keller. Anne and Helen made little progress until Anne convinced Captain and Mrs. Keller that she and Helen had to be separated from them. Anne needed to have full authority over Helen to get her to mind first—and only then could she focus on Helen's education.

Similarly, after a couple of months seeing the Riedels once a week, I realized I needed to work alone with Bert. Deaf-blind people don't function well in group activities. Unless the activities are well coordinated with the right support services for the deaf-blind people, there's no way for them to follow all the action. Even with an interpreter giving them details, they can get left behind sometimes, in the fast-moving pace of sighted and hearing people. I was becoming increasingly uncomfortable trying to manage a lesson for the three Riedels together, so finally I told John and Mary about my concerns: Bert's needs were separate from theirs. He lost focus after about thirty minutes. Maybe I could see Bert first, then meet with them afterward, I proposed.

When John and Mary accepted right away, I was surprised. I hadn't expected a solution to come so easily. But they were problem solvers. I soon realized I'd been struggling needlessly. After this change, Bert and I began working comfortably at our own pace. John and Mary met with me when Bert and I were finished.

Our separate lessons proved a smart move. With one-on-one communication, Bert and I pushed forward unhindered. I plotted my strategy to ensure that he experienced success during each lesson, using words that were easy to remember, with lots of repetition. It wasn't alarming to me when he forgot signs. More often, I was pleasantly surprised when he remembered them. Purposefully, I avoided teaching the fingerspelled alphabet in the early stages. People often struggle to read fingerspelling, and I didn't want Bert to get discouraged early or give up altogether. As he progressed, the time came for teaching the family the whole fingerspelled alphabet.

Bert already knew many of the letters because of signs I'd taught him that incorporate the initial letter. He knew the letter *f* from the word *family.* Each hand forms the *f* handshape, then simultaneously the hands move out and around to make a circle. And he knew *r* because *restroom* and *ready* use that handshape. To the beginner, some of the symbols seem odd. For instance, the letter *s* is a fist, and the letter *g* is the thumb and index finger extended parallel from the fist. It can take months to become fluent at fingerspelling. With time and practice, however, reading fingerspelling can become as easy as reading a book.

I introduced the manual alphabet starting just where you'd expect—with the letter *a.* I proceeded slowly and methodically to letter *z.* Bert inevitably froze up when I tried to rush him with my signing. Even though he knew what letter was coming next, he still savored the feel of every letter before moving on to the next. We practiced

the alphabet over and over. John and Mary practiced
with him every night and in the mornings before I came
in for lessons. They were model students. With fingerspelling behind us, I was able to use the braille machine
less and less with Bert to present or explain new signs. I
could now fingerspell them.

One day I introduced *understand*. "This is u-n-d-e-r-
s-t-a—"

He repeated the letters out loud and put together the
word he thought it was. "U-d-e-r. Udder," he said.

"No." I spelled again, u-n-d-e-r-s-t-a-n-d. It was a long
word. Sometimes he got lost in the fingerspelling when the
words were long and would quit reading before I was done.

"U-n-d-e-r—, oh, *under*." He waited for me to show
him the sign for *under*. Of course, that was not where I
was going. The signs for *under* and *understand* are totally
unrelated.

"No." Again, I spelled u-n-d-e-r-s-t-a-n-d. I loved this
challenge and had the patience for repetition in the teaching setting, but I imagined it was trying for the family to
stay with it all the time until Bert got it. I sensed that Bert
had been accustomed to taking conversations wherever he
wanted. His family and friends must have given in rather
than tried to press him because they simply didn't have
time to pursue correcting him, or they didn't know how.

This time he followed me through to the end of the
word. "Understand," he said.

"Yes," I signed. I pulled his hand by the wrist with
my free hand, up to my temple where I flicked my right
index finger up from a closed fist, giving him the sign for
understand.

Bert was inexperienced at following the movement
of signs, unlike people who were born deaf and became

blind later. If I didn't actually pull his hand along with the movement of my sign, he would be left lost in space. Bert felt my finger motion and thought about it before imitating me, putting his own fist to his temple and flicking out his pinky finger, the same way a young child might have done. I reached up, gently folded his pinky finger down, and pulled his index finger up instead. I showed him again on me.

"I got it," he said, and imitated it perfectly. I could almost see the wheels turning in his mind. "Like a light bulb coming on," he said.

"Yes, right," I signed with a big grin.

Kinda Pokey

The first milestone in working with Bert came about eight weeks into our lessons. It happened while John and Mary were away at their mountain condo for a couple of days. Rather than go with them, Bert preferred staying at home where he was comfortable and self-sufficient. A few days earlier, John had told me that they'd be gone but asked if I would still come over for Bert's lesson.

"How will he know I'm here?" I asked John, knowing that Bert wouldn't hear the doorbell when I arrived.

"He'll have the door unlocked for you," John said.

"Won't I scare him when I just come walking in?"

"Yeah, probably, but he'll be expecting you."

I was excited about this lesson. My plan was to use the time to enlighten Bert about the deaf population to whom he had never been exposed. His deafness linked him to this special group by a common thread woven around distinct communication preferences.

While I described the various communication methods used by deaf persons, I would teach him about the group within the deaf population referred to as the "Deaf community," the native users of American Sign Language. They use the capital *D* in the word *Deaf to* signify the difference between themselves and those who became deaf after acquiring speech, or between those who were raised in the oral method who align themselves more with hearing people. I would explain that their language is a rich and full language—not just like English shorthand, as many people think. ASL has syntax, structure, and clear grammatical features.

In addition to their unique language, the Deaf community has its own social clubs, religious groups, national and state organizations, and competitive sports. There is even a Deaf Olympics. In this culture, Deaf people have accepted codes of behavior different from the hearing world, such as blinking lights on and off in a crowded room to signal that someone has an announcement, or waving one's hand, stamping on the floor, and banging on the table to get an individual's attention. These things that hearing people consider rude are necessary forms of communication in a deaf world.

Unlike spoken languages where there are euphemisms, abstract concepts, and things implied, sign communication is innocently direct and concrete. In the hearing world, where it might be socially unacceptable to mention something like someone's weight gain, it would be matter-of-factly "shown" in sign language.

When two deaf strangers meet, there's usually an immediate connection and sharing of information about themselves using their common language. Even two deaf people from different countries who use two distinct signed languages have a natural inclination to communicate. And they do so by gestures. They have an advantage over foreigners who are not deaf, whose communication is paralyzed when they cannot speak each other's language.

Deaf people are usually eager to meet other deaf people, or people who can sign. They introduce themselves by fingerspelling their own names and then offer their name signs, which are quicker and easier to use. Name signs are typically created by others and given to us. They often depict one of our personal traits, like curly hair, a dimple, or big ears—another example of the direct and concrete nature of the visual language.

I would tell Bert that in my work as an interpreter some people prefer that I use ASL and others prefer Signed English. And then there are other deaf people who don't sign at all but only read lips. Interpreters call them "oral deaf."

Only about ten percent of deaf people are skilled lipreaders. Even among those, a great amount of guess-work goes on, as only thirty to forty percent of the English language is visible on the lips. Many words look alike, for example: *pat* and *bat; thirteen* and *thirty; bad, pad,* and *mad;* and *man* and *pan.* A lipreader, or speech-reader, must have a strong language and knowledge base to begin with to predict what the speaker might be talking about. By narrowing the possibilities of topics to the situation, it increases the speech-reader's chances of understanding.[11]

One deaf woman I know is a highly skilled speech-reader. She told me about a time when she was awakened by her hearing boyfriend who had come in late from work. She didn't know he had stopped off at the pool hall on his way home. Sleepily she asked him, "How did your day go?"

"I beat myself at pool twice," he replied.

She looked surprised and puzzled. "You made your-self a bowl of rice?"

They were able to laugh at her lipreading error that night and other times besides that. The errors could be funny; however, they sometimes led to confusion and misunderstandings—like the time a waitress asked her and her deaf male friend if everything was all right. Her friend assumed the waitress was asking if he would like anything else and he answered *no*. Again, this situation was of minor consequence, but the implication is that others can become disastrous. When the errors have to do with misunderstanding instructions from a doctor or an employer, they can lead to health complications or problems on the job.

The hearing people at my assignments often ask me if the deaf person can read lips. I always refer their question to the deaf consumer. It's too risky for me to make assumptions about what a deaf person can understand by this method, as some deaf people are more skilled than others. There are those who can understand only simple phrases that are in context with an immediate situation. For example, if a person was in a kitchen where someone says, "Bring me a pan," the speech-reader could assume that the correct word is *pan* and not *man*.

When a deaf person is a skilled speech-reader, it seems most of the burden of communication goes onto the deaf person. The hearing person doesn't have to do anything besides continue to speak normally. The speech-reader has the eye-fatiguing work of staring at faces, interpreting lip movements, catching nuances of muscle twitches and body language, all in a task of putting together a verbal puzzle. In a group, speakers are often butting in and talking over each other. By the time a speech-reader has located the person who is talking, that person is finished and someone else has begun speaking. All is lost to the speech-reader—unbeknownst to the group who, after all, believes that the deaf participant can "read lips."

In a classroom, if the deaf student sits up front to be able to speech-read the teacher, the student is frustrated to find the teacher not only walking around the room while lecturing but also turning toward the blackboard to write while speaking. Speech-reading skills are of great value in getting along in the hearing world, yet they are not the panacea the hearing world thinks they are.

I had many thoughts to share with Bert about the deaf population. When I arrived for this special lesson, his classical music greeted me as I let myself into the house. Slinking down into a wicker chair across from where he played, I absorbed the sounds for a few minutes before I approached him. I studied him as he played, unaware of me. In blue tennis shoes, he gently pressed the foot pedal at all the appropriate intervals. The piece was lovely, though I didn't know what it was. When he finished, he startled as usual when I patted his arm.

"Hellooo," he said. "That was Wagner's "Tannhauser." I love that one," he added with zeal. "How *are* you?"

After a hug, we shuffled together over to the kitchen table. Bert was already into an animated monologue when we sat down. His white eyebrows, thin at the temples with unruly hairs toward the bridge of his nose, moved with his expressions, unlike the fixed stare of his eyes. His face lacked the deep wrinkles that would have given away his age, and when he laughed, he looked years younger than eighty-six. His hands didn't look their age either, except for the right index finger that was permanently bent a bit sideways at the top knuckle from years of reading braille.

As Bert was talking, I looked away from him for a minute to the power brailler and realized the computer was not booted up and the braille display was not on. A stir of panic fluttered in my chest. I didn't know how to hook up the machines. My lesson was packed with information.

How could I convey all that I had prepared without the brailler? His sign vocabulary was still not much more than fifty words. How could we have the conversation I had planned without it?

I signed to Bert, "How t-u-r-n on?" Then I set his hand on the machine.

"Oh, I don't know," he said. Computers were not something of his generation. He'd never even seen one before. I was wondering what I was going to do. He suggested we call John to ask him how to turn on the machine. "Yes, sure," I said aloud to myself. "Let's do that."

"Where your phone?" I signed.

"It's on the kitchen counter."

My eyes quickly scanned over the counters. "No, Bert, it's not," I thought out loud. He stood up from the table and used his cane to find his way to the kitchen. He felt across the counters with his hand, assuring me the phone was there. It wasn't.

"Maybe it's in the living room," he said, turning and leading us into the next room. His white cane extended forward. I spotted the phone on the floor near the far side of the gray-and-white-striped couch and bent down to pick it up.

"I have phone," I signed.

"Are you talking to Johnny?"

"No. What phone number?"

"I don't know."

Of course he wouldn't know the phone number, I realized. He doesn't use the phone. I continued searching and found some papers on the desk with notes to me from John and Mary. The phone number for the condo was written there. I informed Bert, "I have phone number." I dialed the number but had no luck reaching John or Mary.

Putting the phone down, I took a deep breath and resigned to switch to plan B, whatever that would be.

"Did you get John?" he asked.

"No," I signed, a little disappointed.

"Oh, we don't need that machine," Bert said.

I found out he was right. Although it was slow and we didn't get to talk about all that I had wished, we had little problem conversing that day. Using the limited sign vocabulary he had, combined with a lot of fingerspelling into his hand, he was able to grasp my intentions. I used elementary phrases to describe the differences between people born deaf and people who became deaf later and how this difference might affect their competencies in English.

Bert understood the gist of my statements and expanded upon them himself. We talked about how blindness requires adaptations in sign language communication, since the facial expressions so essential in the language are not accessible. Having no previous exposure to deaf people or sign language, Bert was becoming more and more curious. He was impressed to learn that sign language is the third most used language in the United States.[12] He strained to imagine hands in fluid motion creating this picturesque language.

Bert was pensive. "Isn't it a lot easier to learn sign language when you can see?" he asked with a chuckle. He told me he was looking forward to the future, to when he would be communicating in sign language with other deaf people. At the same time, I detected some apprehension when he asked if I thought deaf people would look down on him for being blind as well. "Do you think I'm kinda pokey?" he asked.

His questions touched me. Before our session ended, I reassured Bert that deaf people would be understanding and even impressed that he was making an effort to learn sign language. I left him that afternoon feeling gratified with what we had been able to accomplish—and we did it without the machine. All the while, I knew that from a cultural perspective, Bert would have little in common with other deaf people. He had not grown up in their world. The likelihood of him developing strong friendships of that sort was slim.

I drove away thinking about the differences between Bert and those who are born deaf. Whether they attended a deaf residential school or were mainstreamed into a regular classroom, it was common that deaf people preferred to spend time with others like themselves, in an environment where communication was easy and where they shared the same social mores and the same culture. Deaf persons don't consider themselves handicapped, and most are proud of their Deaf identity.

Bert did not share their identity. He was not "Deaf." He was a hearing, speaking person who could no longer hear. He just needed sign language to receive information. He benefited most by relationships with people who understood deafness, could sign, and who were good listeners. Loquacious and social, Bert needed friends and relationships, yet he lacked the ability to make signs himself. Although I held the dream that Bert might someday have conversations and friendships with other signers including deaf people, it was premature to expect it. In fact, I felt sadness that it might never happen.

Futility

A deaf person is more alone among hearing people than he is when he is alone.

— LEO JACOBS, *A Deaf Adult Speaks Out*

Over time I began to know the Riedel family better. I learned the story behind Bert's coming to Colorado and the circumstances that led up to my involvement. When I first met Bert, ten months had passed since he'd lost his wife, Helen, after fifty-eight years of marriage. He'd only been in Colorado for eight months, coming from Oakland, California. He lived there with Helen since 1979. Their home wasn't far from three of their four children, Sue, Marcia, and Philip.

"We moved there from Lombard, Illinois, when the snowy driveways became too much for us," Bert told me. "We wanted to be near our grown children in a warmer climate. Helen picked out our house, which was high on the hill, because she loved the marvelous views. She described the sunsets to me. You could see the San Francisco Bay from our deck. On clear days, looking northwest, you could see the peak of Mount Tamalpais, north of San Francisco, and the hills of Marin County. If you sat on the front porch, you could look down the hill at night and see all the lights of Oakland." Bert described the scenery as if he had seen it himself.

Jake, Bert's grandson, also had fond memories of going to the house in Oakland. He shared them with me in a letter after I asked Bert's family for stories about their past.

"Growing up, Mom [Marcia] and I would make what now seems like weekly pilgrimages from our home in Piedmont to Grandpa and Grandma's house in the hills. Grandpa and Grandma would have cheese and crackers waiting for us. For my mom, this was an opportunity to relax, play cards, and spend some quality time with her mother and father. For me, the budding little capitalist, there was the added appeal of earning a few dollars helping with chores around the house."

Usually, it was Jake helping Bert tend to the garden. Bert was always prepared, having the gardening tools laid out neatly on a glass-topped table on the front deck. "He'd hand me a pair of gardening gloves and we would take a slow walk around the garden while Grandpa described what needed to be done: pruning, weeding, and planting," Jake said.

With a mouth full of cheese and crackers, Jake would begin his gardening chores. He would work alone for a while and then Bert would join him. Wearing an old baseball cap and gardening gloves, Bert would approach with pruning shears, an empty cardboard box, and one of his usual cheery *hellooo's*.

Jake recalled how Bert gathered the clippings and weeds and methodically cut them into manageable pieces before putting them into the box. When the box was full, he emptied it into the garbage can and started filling the box up again. Jake could easily have taken care of the grass clippings himself. He watched admiringly as Bert managed to do the work that one might not expect a blind and nearly deaf person to do. For Bert, this was just another daily challenge he was determined to meet. Although his grandpa really needed the help, Jake liked to think the real reason Bert put on his old baseball cap and gardening gloves was to spend more time with his grandson.

When the yard work was finished, Bert and Jake would head into the house where they would sit and drink Pepsi from tall glasses. Jake liked listening to Bert describe what he was reading in *National Geographic,* and Jake liked talking about what he was doing in school and how his swimming season was progressing. Then Jake would help himself to a grape Popsicle from the freezer and slowly consume it over a game of cards with Grandma Helen. Riding back home to Piedmont, he was already looking forward to his next visit.

Despite their lovely house and spectacular views, the retirement years in Oakland were not all what Bert and Helen had hoped for. Bert's blindness and deafness had progressed to the point where he was no longer able to communicate with any friends. He was further isolated because he could no longer walk alone as he had on the streets of Lombard. The uneven terrain of the hills was too unpredictable to maneuver alone, even with his cane or if he had a guide dog.

Helen had joined a women's club, and for a time enjoyed some friendships until her health problems started interfering with her social life. Her continuous bouts with emphysema resulted in numerous hospitalizations, and Bert, worrying about her safety, convinced her to give up driving. "She wasn't happy about that, but it had to be," he told me with a shrug.

For many years the family had been adapting to Bert's vision loss. Now the hearing loss proved to be the most difficult. At family gatherings everyone had to speak loudly into the hearing aid microphone in Bert's pocket for him to try to decipher what they were saying. The attempts at communicating proved futile, since most of the time Bert misinterpreted the bits of sounds that he could hear and got the information all mixed up. "When Dad didn't understand, we had to say it louder and louder until it turned into this screaming thing," John told me. "It was like we were all angry, but we didn't start out that way. Everyone felt the tension."

"Dad, this is Lindsey," Marcia would say, trying to introduce her niece.

"Hello, Alison, nice of you to come." Bert would say, unable to tell his own grandchildren apart. "No, it's Lindsey," Marcia and Lindsey would yell together, "Lindsey!"

"How are you Alison? Good. That's wonderful." He answered his own questions. It seemed everyone knew he had it all turned around, except himself. They would give up in exasperation. There was just no way to get information across to him. It became a one-way communication, with Bert doing all the talking. At one point, his daughter Sue recognized the seriousness of the barrier and recommended they all learn sign language. Bert couldn't perceive how he would be able to learn sign language. He still thought he was getting by well enough. Unfortunately, with everyone's attention on Helen's illness, no one was in a position to act on Sue's suggestion.

Dealing with the problems, the children supported their parents as much as possible. Marcia drove her mother to her increasingly frequent medical appointments, Phil took hikes with his father, and Sue made sure various other needs were met. But mostly it was Bert and Helen taking care of each other. She was his eyes and ears and he was her mobility. Bert would pull Helen backward in the wheelchair around the house, feeling his way along the walls and doorways, as that was how he navigated without sight. Finally, a woman was hired to come in during the week to help with the cooking and cleaning. Bert and Helen managed by themselves on the weekends.

Tending to Helen's weakening condition, Bert neglected his own health, developing digestive ailments and swelling in his ankle. Together, he and Helen were confined to the house. In the final stages of her disease, she had so much trouble speaking, she was left to resort to a crude touch language with Bert, consisting of three signals: *yes, no*, and *I don't know*. Bert's concerns mounted. "We just stayed home and Helen would sit in the chair while we played cards. We didn't go out or visit our children because it was too hard on Helen."

Every day, the two of them sat with Bert's brailled deck of cards playing their favorite honeymoon bridge. Sometimes Bert would turn on the radio or the TV for Helen, but she really wasn't interested in them. She went to bed after lunch. Finally, even the bridge games became too much for her. She was struggling to breathe. "We were losing our lives," Bert lamented.

The Value of Braille

John and Mary had been living in Colorado for three years before Bert moved in. They had moved from West Chicago, Illinois, where they'd both grown up, because they loved the Colorado mountains. When they bought the house in Conifer, it was with John's father in mind. In spite of the communication difficulties over many years since Bert became legally blind and increasingly deaf, they'd had an understanding with him that if anything ever happened to Helen, he was welcome to live with them. They thought the newly built home would be just right for the three of them.

John established a new business as a health-care consultant while Mary did his bookkeeping and managed their home office. They joined the Colorado Mountain Club to explore the Rocky Mountains and became involved with the Mountain Resource Center, an agency that serves area residents who need temporary emergency resources. Mary was learning about high-altitude gardening and doing some landscaping on their property. Their social activities and traveling were taking up the rest of their time.

As Helen's health continued to deteriorate, it became more likely that Bert would be moving to Colorado. Even at his advanced age and with his profound disability, a nursing home or assisted living didn't seem like options to John and Mary. They knew Bert was still clinging to a zest for life—a zest that the stress and strain of the past few years had nearly extinguished.

The communication problem of so many years had contributed to much of the strain. For the past seven years, however, it had eased partly with the help of new technology. When they lived in West Chicago, John and Mary had purchased a translator program for the computer and a Blazie Braille printer that enabled them to correspond with Bert through braille letters. It was a blessing. Finally, Bert could share in his kids' lives. Now, instead of being left out, Bert could be first to receive news. He could read their letters to Helen. From Colorado, John and Mary continued sending letters and extended the offer of their home.

While Bert considered moving in with them, he asked if they had any steps. One thing he was afraid of was steps. Unfortunately, there were fifteen, they said. Nevertheless, John and Mary had some fresh energy and new ideas and felt they could make a difference in Bert's life. They thought that with a modest addition to their house, there would be plenty of room. He could have a comfortable apartment there.

Bert was still considering the idea in May of 1997 when John and Mary flew to California to visit him. Helen was gravely ill, and everyone knew she didn't have long to live. Bert, prepared for her passing, revealed to them, "All my life I've maintained my independence, never intending to be a burden on my children, but Helen has strongly suggested I take you up on your offer to come live with you."

His children wondered how Helen ever got that suggestion across to him because she could barely speak above a whisper and he couldn't hear a thing. They assumed it had been Bert's own internal thought process and maybe some of Helen's tapping of *yes* and *no* answers to his questions that brought him to this conclusion. Whichever way it was, John and Mary accepted Bert's proposal without hesitation. With Bert's decision made about where he would live and the fact that Helen had seen all of her children recently, she slipped away during John and Mary's visit. Bert didn't hear her last words. Mary told him later that Helen had simply said, "I love you, Bert."

The memorial service was held a few weeks later in Piedmont, near Oakland. The morning before the service Bert sat with his younger brother, Hank, on the back deck of the house. Other family members were gathered close by. "Bert," Hank said, touching his younger brother's arm.

"Who is this?" Bert responded.

"Hank—it's your brother, Hank," he shouted.

"Is this John?"

"No, I'm Hank."

"Hank?"

"Yes. The Haleys—"

"What is it? Is it time to eat?"

"No, Bert, the Haleys send—"

"There's a lot of people here, aren't there? I'm sure it's going to be a lovely service," Bert said.

John interrupted to assist Hank. Bert felt hands from a new direction. "Hellooo. Who is it?"

"Dad, it's John."

"Is this Johnny?"

"Yes, Dad. The Haleys want you to know they send their condolences." The Haleys were mutual friends of Bert and Hank's.

"I smell the food. I guess we'll be eating soon," Bert said. Mary and Philip tried to tell Bert about the Haleys, too, but he never did understand what they were saying.

Times like this increased the family's appreciation for the value of braille. It was the only way to reach Bert. After the memorial, while John and Mary were flying home, Marcia met with a representative of a company in Oakland who sold PowerBraille Display units to see about getting one. They'd tested one of these machines a year earlier at Bert's house. Miraculously, it had made communication possible, but Bert didn't want to buy one. The device was costly because it was a new technology with limited demand. Many deaf-blind people didn't read braille, didn't know about the machines, or just couldn't afford them. At that time Bert didn't see the necessity for something that cost thousands of dollars. It seemed like an extravagant purchase. He'd been strongly independent and was unwilling to let go of the pretence he had held onto for so long—that he was managing fine. He thought he could still hear "good enough."

However, when it became inevitable that Bert would be moving to Colorado, John and Mary insisted they have the machine. Bert's reluctance to buy it was overpowered by his longing for meaningful communication. The machine could break him out of the isolation he'd been in for so long. He acquiesced and bought the device.

In Conifer, John and Mary began constructing the addition to their house. Other preparations had to be made as well to customize the whole house to Bert's blindness before he could move in. At a store that sells adaptive equipment for blind and deaf persons, they purchased new braille playing cards and an electronic doorbell with a pager that vibrates when callers arrive. They picked out a large wall clock on which they pasted braille numbers, and they bought a braille embosser to make braille labels. They labeled everything including clothes, cabinets, and cleaning products. Additionally, a woman was hired to help in the kitchen and another one to help with the housekeeping.

Then, still grieving two months after the loss of Helen, Bert arrived with his daughter Sue at Denver International Airport. Walking on the side of his foot, his ankle the size of an orange, Bert brought all of his health problems along with his social isolation. Life for Bert, John, and Mary was about to change, but none of them knew how dramatically.

The plan was for them to stay in downtown Denver for a couple of nights so Bert could acclimate slowly to the higher altitude. Then they would move up to Conifer and see how he did at 8,500 feet elevation. At the Hyatt Hotel they rested at first, until Mary thought to take Bert to the pool. She knew he loved to swim and this would be a good transition to his new home. From the poolside she watched him touching the sidewall ever so slightly with each stroke through the water, guiding himself slowly back and forth. At the end of several laps he stood up in the pool, surprising her when he threw his hands into the air and exclaimed, "I'm so happy to be here. I'm going to live with my son, John, and Mary." His joy brought tears to her eyes.

A walk downtown the next morning assured them he wasn't suffering from any signs of altitude sickness. Bert said he was ready to go "home" to Conifer, so they checked out of the hotel and headed home, a day earlier than planned.

The first days together were, to say the least, challenging. Bert had to be oriented to his new surroundings. This meant going over every inch of space in his bedroom, his sitting room, his bathroom, and the upstairs, over and over and more times again. He counted the steps to each chair and table as John and Mary took turns leading him from one to the other. He memorized the location of every doorway and each piece of furniture. Nothing could be moved from its place after that. The training continued for months.

The slightest miscalculation on his part would aim him in the wrong direction. If he left from the doorway to his bedroom off angle, he would run into the piano instead of his sitting chair. Then, very confused, he had difficulty finding his way back to his bedroom from where he needed to start all over. A door, a table, or chair could feel totally different from a new angle, and he would be lost in his own house. Such being the case, it was a touching moment for John and Mary when they found Bert practicing his navigating on his own, well after he'd already told them, "Good night." Watching him from outside his apartment, they swelled with pride at his diligence.

Just like new parents, they were always keeping an eye open and an ear out for Bert's safety. One day, not long after Bert had moved in, they were working in the yard when they heard a low muffled howl. They stood still for a few moments, listening carefully to figure it out. "It sounds like a cry for help," Mary said throwing down her rake. John dropped his tools, too, as they sped into the house. The sound was coming from the upstairs. There they found Bert, stuck in Mary's office, a place he'd never explored before. He hadn't recognized any landmarks and couldn't find the door to get out. After about an hour he sat down on the floor and resigned himself to calling out for help.

The power brailler provided a breakthrough into the family's communication quandary. The machine allowed

Bert to hear from others at last. He was participating in the immediate action instead of sitting on the sidelines, imagining what everyone else might be doing or saying. This new experience, however, was not without challenges. It took many months for each of them to learn how to communicate on the machine. For years, Bert had been accustomed to doing all the talking. Now he could be a listener as well, but that skill would take time to develop. Often Bert would read only half a sentence on the brailler before responding and the conversation would then go into taxing directions.

One day, Bert read as John typed, "'We want to let you know we're going—' Oh, you're going out. I see. I'll see you in a little while then."

"No, we're not going now—"

"Oh, you're going in a little while, I see."

"No, I mean we will be going—"

"I see. You're going out later. That's fine."

"No, we are going on a vacation."

"A vacation? Now?"

"No, we're planning a vacation in six months." The conversations were time-consuming. Communicating by typed words takes much longer than spoken conversations. A spoken thought that takes two seconds requires several minutes in braille to include the entire context necessary to capture the meaning. It took longer if Bert interrupted mid-sentence and more time when he took the conversation in a different direction from where the typist intended. Thoughts didn't always translate exactly when they were typed out in real time, and misunderstandings were frequent. Sometimes the conversation became so confused that the typist gave up and moved on.

With time and practice, the misunderstandings between the three of them became fewer and fewer. Using the machine, Bert was able to take part in conversations at the dinner table. Marcia, Sue, Philip, and Bert's brother Hank called him on the phone and John transmitted their words through the brailler. Mary told him the plans for the day and sometimes for the whole week. She asked him questions and described events. They included him in decision-making, something the family couldn't do for years. Bert was aware of this significant change. "I'm finally in the club," he exclaimed.

They lugged the power brailler everywhere the three of them went—even to Mount Evans. It was about an hour's drive from their home to the entrance of the Arapahoe National Forest. One morning, they stopped at the little stone building to pay the fee before starting up the fourteen-mile byway to the summit. John drove while Mary sat in the backseat typing on the laptop. Bert sat in front. As they began their ascent through the pine forest, Mary described the "highest paved road in America." Bert held the brailler on his lap seeing the scenery in his mind as she portrayed it. Carloads of hikers stopped at various parking areas along the way to the summit to explore the trails. John continued past them, steering the Jeep around hairpin curves on the two-lane road. Helmeted bikers in striped racing gear sped down the lane opposite them.

Bert felt the Jeep maneuver the tight switchbacks. "This is a winding road," he said. He appreciated Mary's excitement about the steep drop-offs next to the road with views that stole her breath. "We're halfway to the top," she typed. "We're in Cloudland. The clouds are heavy, falling below us, and the cliff walls tower overhead. John is looking out toward the craggy cliffs to scout for bighorn sheep."

"Ooooh, can you imagine that? Bighorn sheep," Bert said.

They neared the summit above timberline. Smells of burning rubber from cars braking on their descents lingered as they passed them. "There are marmots scurrying along the rocks next to the road. They're brown and fat," Mary typed. "They look like skinny beavers, only they have long furry tails. One is splayed out, on a flat rock watching the motorists pass by. There're no more pine trees up here, only groves of bristlecone pines. Some of them are more than a thousand years old. They're unusual looking, with light brown twisted trunks and bushy outcroppings of green needles at the top."

Then there were no trees at all, only rocks and mountain grasses with yellow and white wildflowers and patches of snow. The rocks looked like they could come sliding down onto the narrow road lined with slow-moving cars. The road soon became the only entity among the rocks and sky. John stopped the Jeep before they got to the summit parking lot. "We have mountain goats right outside our car," Mary typed. "You can touch them if you want to. Put your hand out the window." The shaggy white goats with long faces and dark eyes obliged them by standing still. "Ooooh, they're tame," Bert said, as he petted one.

At the summit, they got out and took a walk. Without the brailler John and Mary couldn't tell Bert about the crowd of people that seemed to be crawling onto the higher rocks. Some people were so high up on the massive pile of rocks that they looked only two inches tall. Bert couldn't see the vast expanse of purple mountains surrounding them: Mount Bierstadt, Grays and Torreys Peaks to the west, Longs Peak to the north, and Pikes Peak to the south. Lake-dotted basins were tucked far down in between the peaks. John and Mary could see more than one hundred miles in every direction. Bert felt the rock formations, the arctic tundra, and sniffed a few wildflowers.

In spite of the late summer month, the thin air was cold at 14,264 feet. A few lurking thunder clouds cast shadows upon the barren hills. The three of them shivered as they sat together on a rock drinking hot soup from a thermos.

A Neon Sign

The welcome to Colorado and the new two-way communication was helping Bert to go forward. Everyone was happy about that. He'd adapted to many changes in his life and to considerable losses. Helen's passing was the most difficult change he'd ever faced, and this sadness overwhelmed him at times. He went about his activities, but he missed Helen. It broke John and Mary's hearts every day when they found him crying.

Sensitive to his delicate condition, they pushed on, trying to improve the situation. John's light humor had a way of lifting his dad out of his slumps and Mary bought him new clothes. "People here wear fleece," she said. Bert hadn't thought anything was wrong with his old clothes. His fading vision didn't pick out the worn places on the clothing that felt good and familiar to him. Mary selected smart corduroys with matching shirts and labeled each one with embossed braille tags so he could choose his own clothes in the mornings.

They addressed Bert's health problems by starting him on a walking program, hiking with him daily around their neighborhood. Mary hired a physical trainer to teach Bert how to use their home gym equipment. And they made trips to the recreation center to go swimming. During this rehabilitation of his physical health, John and Mary also sought ways to stimulate Bert's social life.

They decided to invite all of their new Colorado friends and neighbors to a summer open house so Bert could meet them and everyone could learn how to use the braille machine. At his request, Mary asked each person to write something about themselves and send it to them in advance. John and Mary would braille the information for Bert because he was interested in knowing a little about each person before he actually met them. He wanted to have something to talk about with them. Carrie and Jack were two of the neighbors invited.

Before they came to the open house, Carrie called the Riedels and mentioned that Jack's niece, a certified teacher for the blind in southern Illinois, would be visiting them that weekend. Shana visited Colorado each summer when she drove her grandparents out to visit Jack, their son. Carrie asked if the Riedels would be interested in meeting Shana. John and Mary were open to any new opportunity for Bert. They said yes, of course, so Shana was invited to the party, too.

The day of the open house, Carrie was amazed that Bert remembered everything she'd written. "He had a charming sense of humor," she said after I first became acquainted with her, "and almost immediately after that I began visiting him regularly to play honeymoon bridge. We got along well because he liked to talk and I'm a good listener."

Shana, who Bert hadn't received information from earlier, met him at the open house. Using the braille machine, she informed him that as an itinerant teacher, she traveled between twenty-five schools. She supervised a case load of blind students, some of whom were also deaf and used sign language. Amidst various and boisterous conversations, Shana sat with Bert, blocking out the commotion while she typed a description of the deaf-blind children who used sign language. Bert acted interested in the children and asked lots of questions. Shana responded, surprised that Bert *only* used braille to communicate and not tactile sign. It puzzled her that a man with such intellect had never learned to sign. "Bert," she said, "you need to learn sign language."

While he was interested in hearing about her students who used sign, Bert was resistant to using sign language himself. He thought he was too old to learn it. It seemed too monumental a task. Shana, however, was not convinced that Bert was too old. She saw no deficiencies with his mind and observed how active he was. She thought his age was a weak excuse. Before the afternoon was over, she briefly explained tactile sign language to John and Mary, emphasizing that it would open many more doors to Bert. Shana suspected they hadn't thought it possible for Bert to learn sign language either, but now Mary wanted to know more. She invited Shana and Carrie to come back the next day, Monday, to discuss it further.

When Shana spoke with Bert again on Monday, he hadn't changed his mind. He maintained he still had enough hearing to get by and didn't think sign language was necessary. This was the same thing he'd told the family years before, when his daughter Sue had brought the subject up. He didn't know how he would go about learning sign language anyway.

Mary had been in the kitchen tending to refreshments during Bert's visit with Shana. At the end of their conversation, she overheard him concede to Shana, "It might not be a bad idea." Instantly, Mary bounded outside to the deck where Carrie and John were talking. Full of emotion she shouted, "He agreed . . . he agreed that learning sign language might not be a bad idea."

*Bert and Rocky, outside on the front porch awaiting a
friendly visitor from the Mountain Resource Center.*

Shana had obviously made an impression on Bert.
Before leaving the Riedels, she offered to assist them with
whatever resources they might need. That offer would stay
at the forefront of their minds as they continued to explore
ways to enhance Bert's quality of life.

Through John and Mary's affiliation with the Mountain
Resource Center, they found other volunteers to play
bridge with Bert and to take him swimming. One of them
was Vera Feistel, a gifted high school student. Vera had gotten involved in the Mountain Resource Center to expand
her horizons beyond school activities. When she heard
about Bert, she eagerly jumped for the opportunity of
learning to play bridge with a deaf-blind senior citizen. Just

curious at first, she was rapidly fascinated, finding Bert quite the opposite of her preconceived notion of what elderly people were like. And Bert liked Vera. He enjoyed her soft style and her fresh enthusiasm for life. Soon they were spending time together weekly.

Vera took Bert on walks. Afterward, at the braille machine, they engaged in talks, like granddaughter and granddad. They discussed Mother Teresa and Eleanor Roosevelt and Bert expounded on his philosophy of life. Bert taught Vera to play honeymoon bridge. Eventually he would come to teach her other lessons about life.

• • • • •

As autumn was well under way, Mary continued to adroitly manage Bert's schedule, filling in all the gaps of the calendar. The weekly swimming, weight training, and the resurgence of social contacts eased some of his sadness of missing Helen. Medication had helped resolve his digestive disorder, and physical therapy along with a new orthotic device in his shoe had corrected his ankle problem. Now Bert was energized—ready for even more activity.

In the meantime, John had become aware of the Colorado School for the Deaf and Blind in Colorado Springs, just two hours away. Curious to see what was available there, John and Bert decided to take a trip to the school. Bert was always eager to meet new people and he thought, if nothing else, he could show the children how he played the piano. Maybe they'd never had a deaf-blind adult role model before, he reasoned. So, one October day, they headed toward Colorado Springs.

Traveling south on Interstate 25, the drive took them over Monument Hill where John glimpsed the snow-capped tip of Pikes Peak in the distance. They drove past the shining silver buildings of the Air Force Academy, where the campus of the prestigious school spread out against a backdrop of green and purple mountains. Huge letters, spelling "AIR FORCE" across the seats of the football stadium, caught John's eye, but he was unable to tell his father about any of this beautiful scenery. Instead he just listened to Bert's elongated one-way conversation.

John exited the highway onto Nevada Street in the northern section of Colorado Springs. The throughway led them from an old business district through a residential area of Victorian homes into the center of town. From there they turned onto Kiowa Street, famous for the stretch of crabapple trees lining its median. Mingled with maple and ash, the crabapple leaves painted the Victorian neighborhood with a flood of color. Red, orange, yellow, and brown leaves flittered in the air, down to the ground. Piles of them littered the street. Ahead, at the top of the hill where Kiowa met Institute Street, John could see the roof of an old stone building peeking through the treetops.

When they reached the intersection, thirty-seven acres of campus lay before them. John read the carved wooden sign aloud: "Colorado School for the Deaf and the Blind, established in 1874." Bert's conversation quieted with their Jeep at the stop sign. They were nearing their objective.

John turned onto Institute and followed the white iron fence around to a parking lot on the north side of the school. From there, he led his father inside a newer brick building where they were to meet the principal, David Farrell.

While Bert waited in the administrator's office, he could hear some sounds of John chatting with the principal but didn't know what they were saying. Then Mr. Farrell came over and started some finger movements in Bert's hand. "I didn't know what he was doing," Bert recollected more than a year later. "I was in a bad way."

Bert had sat politely while John and Mr. Farrell finished their meeting. Then he and John followed Mr. Farrell into the computer lab, which housed some of the latest technology for the blind. Unfortunately, because Bert didn't know sign language, Mr. Farrell was unable to communicate to Bert what he was showing John. Afterward he took them to the music room and introduced them to the music teacher. When she shook Bert's hand, he didn't know who it was. Only later, when Bert communicated with John on the braille machine at home, would he understand who he actually met on that visit.

In the music room, John had walked Bert over to one of the two grand pianos near an empty stage where Bert played for them. "I played a little while, but there were no kids there to play for," Bert remembered. "We left after that."

Driving away from the campus, John noticed Pikes Peak again, directly to the west hovering magnificently over the city like a guardian angel. Retracing their route through the residential area, he studied the époque of the Victorian neighborhood a little more carefully. Each home was painted in a different shade of beige, purple, or green. Unaware of those surroundings, Bert sat quietly pensive during the trip home. To Bert, the visit had resulted in nothing significant. In reality, though, just as Shana had done, Mr. Farrell had planted another seed when he spelled into Bert's hand.

• • • • •

On the home front, the revival of Bert's zest for living was picking up speed. John and Mary channeled all of his new energy as fast as he generated it. Meals began to last one to two hours while Bert processed with them the multitude of thoughts on his mind. Doctors' appointments took two to three hours including setting up the braille machine and translating between the doctor and Bert. Trips to the grocery took twice as long, yet sometimes they were twice the fun with Bert having to guess the various products by touching and smelling.

Days at the Riedel home often began as early as 4:30 a.m. Sometimes Bert was up practicing the piano or tapping out letters to Marcia and Philip on his old manual typewriter right outside John and Mary's bedroom door. He began a prolific writing of articles and poetry. John and Mary proofread Bert's works and retyped them into the computer so they could then be printed into braille. Once they were brailled, Bert could read them and retype them with his revisions until they were perfect. The letters to the family didn't need to be reviewed and revised, and the old manual typewriter remained adequate for those that didn't need to be perfect.

For Bert to be fully included in everything, John and Mary wrote vivid descriptions of places they'd been. They even shared conversations they'd recently had with others, converting them into braille. They converted all the letters and articles people sent to Bert. His voracious appetite for correspondence and his interest in every detail and aspect of his world made everyone around him keen to keep giving him more.

This rehabilitation and assimilation of Bert into their life was turning out wonderfully for all three of them. At the same time, John and Mary found it taking them away from work and the life they used to have. Although their determination and perseverance never waned, the couple recognized they were overwhelmed and exhausted. They needed to regain balance in their own lives. For this to happen, they needed Bert to have more independence. So John and Mary increased their efforts to find ways.

The first thing John did was to locate a Perkins Brailler. At the Vocational Rehabilitation Center in Lakewood, he found one of these portable machines that Bert could use to type his poetry directly into braille. The machine was like an old-fashioned manual typewriter but it only had six keys and a space bar. Bert had learned to use a Perkins Brailler more than twenty years earlier in Chicago, when he went through vocational training for the blind. He'd learned all the key-stroke combinations to imprint the characters onto sturdy braille paper. Although this method was slower than regular typing, Bert could manage it independently. It would eliminate the need for another person to retype his work into the computer. The center offered the machine to the Riedels on loan to see if it would fit Bert's needs.

Meanwhile, Mary initiated an arrangement with the local Seniors' Resource Center for Bert to attend their "Yellow House Café," where he could engage in social activities and educational programs with other seniors. Bert agreed to try it, and so volunteers transported him there and tried their hand at interpreting for a deaf-blind man, via the power brailler.

Bert told me a little about his experience at the Yellow House Café. "I met an interesting array of people there," he said. "Mostly women, because they're the ones who like to improve themselves. Men are reluctant to do anything. They had speakers come and talk to us and a lady played the harp, but I couldn't take part in those things. I would have to be quiet and read my braille magazines. There wasn't much for me to do there, though I played the piano some.

It felt like a hospital because the other people had more serious problems than I did."

The group activities at the senior center proved unsatisfying for Bert because they didn't adequately accommodate his deafness and blindness. He couldn't interact with anyone except the staff, and he felt guilty for taking up so much of their time when they had others who needed attention more than he. Bert left the senior center not long after starting, favoring walks and card games back home with Vera and his other friends.

John and Mary's next idea would become more precious than a gemstone. For Father's Day they built Bert a path. They bulldozed the trail down the hill around their mountain property, smoothing out all of the bumps and drop-offs they thought might cause trips and stumbles. Then, with Bert helping to steady the posts, they set one in concrete every twenty feet and connected them with a rope guideline. After they lined the path with soft pine mulch, Bert could walk any time he wished—independently for the first time in thirty years.

The path began right outside the door of his lower-level apartment. Two or three times a day, Bert donned his cap and fleece jacket, making sure he had plenty of doggie treats nestled in his pocket. Holding his cane in one hand, he slid the glass door open with the other and felt for the rope fastened to the side of the house. With the security of the rope, he trod confidently down the 260-foot path with Rocky, the Riedels' black Australian Shepherd/Bernese mountain dog, always at his side. Bert spoke fondly of his path. He even wrote about it. One of his articles was published in *Nat-Cent News,*[13] but before that, he memorized it and recited parts of it to me: "At the end of my path I can sit on my bench and picture the forest that

First independence in forty years; Bert on his path.

John and Mary have described to me. There's a profusion of wildflowers all around and pines covering the ridges. There's a meadow down below where elk graze and, as I face west, there are profound views of the Rocky Mountains. I relish the sun and the fog, the scents, and the breeze."

In many ways, this path was a blessing during the arduous months of the threesome's adjustment to living together. Bert spent many hours enjoying his newfound freedom while John and Mary worked inside and took some time for themselves. He loved to sit on the bench at the end of the path waiting for the changes of weather that brought added excitement to his walks.

Bert and Rocky, enjoying time at Bert's reading bench with a neighbor's dog, Tilly.

Yet with all of this effort, something was still missing. Thorny problems came up when they were out together and couldn't bring the braille machine along. There was no way to ask Bert if he wanted to use the restroom at the mall or to ask if he wanted to buy black shoes or white shoes. They couldn't tell him what was on the menu at the restaurant or ask what he wanted to eat. If they were on a walk, they couldn't tell him there was a snake on the sidewalk, four boats on the lake, or six elk in the field. They couldn't tell him they were stuck in a traffic jam or stopping for gasoline.

In the grocery store, Mary couldn't tell him she'd left her wallet in the car and needed to run back for it. She couldn't abandon him in the store. She'd have to slowly lead him back to the car and leave him wondering, as she hurried back into the store to pay. Often they simply couldn't communicate. At times the frustration escalated and situations seemed insurmountable. One day a letter from Shana arrived. Once again, Shana was imperative about Bert learning sign language. The issue of sign language kept coming up—like a flashing neon sign, refusing to be dismissed.

· · · · ·

"After this letter from Shana, we knew we had to try sign language," Mary remarked one morning after I'd been listening to the family's story for a couple of weeks. She and I were sitting at the small oak table after our morning lesson. The late May sun was beginning to warm the kitchen, and soon Bert would be coming up from his apartment for lunch. He was very precise in keeping to time schedules. "Even then, Bert was hesitant about learning it," Mary continued. "I pleaded with him to try just six lessons."

Although she sensed sign language might help Bert, she knew it wasn't fair to ask him to do all the work alone. Communication was the responsibility of both sides. Mary didn't say to him, *you* need to learn sign language. She said, *we'll* learn it with you. If you don't like it, we can stop. Bert finally agreed, so John and Mary began a search to find someone to teach them. Using every resource they had, they called person after person, looking for the one who could help. Mostly, the response they heard was, "Sign language for an eighty-six-year-old? It can't be done." But Mary was intent. She persisted in calling and would call until she found what she was looking for. Finally, the Helen Keller Regional Center for the Blind in Denver referred her to Barb Coffan, an interpreter from Arvada.

"Barb thought about the long traveling distance between Conifer and Arvada and referred us to you instead," Mary told me, "since you live here." Another door had closed, but as long as others were opening, Mary kept calling until she found me.

I watched her dab at some tears that had spilled over onto her cheeks. I felt them filling my eyes, too. I sensed Mary's relief that someone understood the marathon year they'd been through. I couldn't imagine myself in her shoes, but I did know firsthand from interpreting for deaf-blind people that tactile communication usually takes two to three times longer than ordinary conversation and that interacting with deaf-blind people requires tremendous flexibility, resourcefulness, and patience. Mary and I sat at the table without speaking for a few minutes until we heard sounds of Bert coming up the stairs.

The Essence of Life

Whatever the month, the sun always seemed to shine in the Riedels' house. Fresh and clean throughout, touches of the Southwest decorated their home. An adobe mantel charmed the living room, displaying artifacts from their travels on its shelves. A large framed Aztec photograph of sunrays streaming into a kiva graced the wall above a stone fireplace in the dining room. Everything was kept neatly in place, with nothing left lying around to surprise or trip a blind man.

Outside their home, young aspen trees stood in the meadow filled with early June wildflowers. Mary, who was perpetually managing several tasks at once, welcomed me at the door and took a minute to chat. It had been about three months since my first visit. Bert and I were meeting regularly now, twice a week. My lessons with John and Mary were less structured.

As we stood in the entryway to the kitchen, Mary expressed some new excitement. "Guess what?" she asked. "Dad was singing today."

"Yeah?" I responded with a question in my voice, wondering what was so special about that.

"Do you know what that means?" she asked.

"No, what?"

"It means he's happy. He's not crying and depressed anymore."

I was happy to hear that the cloud of sadness they'd seen hanging over Bert since he'd lost Helen had lifted.

"He's writing a poem for you on his typewriter," she said.

I couldn't remember anyone ever having written a poem for me before, except for one boy during high school. Curiously, I looked forward to seeing what this poem was about, but when I saw Bert, he didn't mention it. Our lessons continued as usual for a couple of weeks without any word from Bert about a poem. Finally Mary asked me, "Did he give you the poem yet?"

"No, not yet."

"He must be waiting until he's got it perfect."

I eagerly anticipated the poem over several more lessons, but it didn't appear. I focused on teaching. Then on the morning of July 3, 1998, while John, Mary, and I were concentrating on a list of new sign vocabulary, we heard Bert ascending the stairs from his apartment. From behind me I could tell when he had emerged from the doorway and was heading toward us. I heard his cane tapping on the wood floor and twisted around in my chair to see him taking careful steps. He was carrying a present. His free arm circled around it. I sensed that John and Mary were in on some secret because they stopped working on their word list. Nobody said anything as we watched Bert approach. He made contact with our table with his cane.

"Hellooo. I have a gift for my teacher," he announced. Proudly, he presented the box to me.

My eyes widened. "It's not even my birthday yet," I said, accepting the gift wrapped in flowered paper. His present was a brown suede bag, suitable for hauling my teaching materials.

"He picked it out himself," Mary said. Inside, I found the poem tucked neatly, along with a shiny red apple. I was touched. "This is so sweet."

He'd typed the poem himself on his old Olympia typewriter. "Dear Diane," it began.

"As we all know, the Declaration of Independence celebrated on July fourth, is a tremendous step forward toward freedom in the field of human rights. In a somewhat similar manner, the transition of those afflicted with sound difficulties, with the aid of professional teachers of sign, is also a step forward to independence in communication. Thus, we thank you for your dedication in your work. The following is a poem in your honor, My Mrs. Chips. In addition to celebrating the Declaration of Independence, I am adding the Declaration of Communication. This poem is the result of the many tips of Mrs. Chips."

Although I am elderly, I have a teacher.
No, she is not a preacher.
Her work is with those with affliction of
 sound,
She tries to help us come around.
Her chuckles are so delightful,
And she makes the work worthwhile.
When I think about the future with her,
 all I can do is smile.

My heart sang at his gesture and expression of gratitude. He had moved on to the piano by then to play for me the tunes he could only feel and remember in his head, never missing a note. He did this at the end of every lesson, maybe slightly aware that as he played, I

Daily music. Bert at his "upstairs" piano.

took away the other gifts he gave me: bits of his positive spirit, his determination, and the things he said that showed me how to see the very essence of life as only one who is deaf and blind can know it.

• • • • •

I got to meet more of Bert's family that month when his daughter Marcia came to visit for a week. She was exactly how I imagined her based upon the family's description—tall, slim, and gracious, with a beautiful smile. She and Mary were getting ready to go for a hike and we were exchanging pleasantries before they left.

The ambiance of the crisp morning air and the surrounding meadow of aspen trees glistening in the early
morning sun enticed me to be outside, and I almost
wished I were going hiking with them. I suspected Marcia
shared her family's appreciation of the mountains. The
scents of pine and wildflowers, so familiar to us mountain
dwellers that we barely noticed them, were distinct from
the coastal air of her California home.

As we talked, Bert was playing Beethoven's "Moonlight
Sonata." When he finished the piece, I ended my chat with
Marcia. The house was quiet after they left. It was just Bert
and me.

After her visit to Colorado, Marcia and I corresponded by letter a few times. From her I got a better
appreciation of how classical music fit into the lives of this
family I had come to know. The sounds of Beethoven,
Brahms, Chopin, and Dvorak had filled her childhood
home when they lived in Maine. At night her mother
often sat at her small desk at the end of the hall, writing
letters or paying bills while her father played his
Chickering upright piano. The piano was on the other
side of the wall from the bedroom Marcia shared with her
older sister, Sue. Safe and snug in their double bed, they
listened to their father play. Many nights the "Moonlight
Sonata" lulled them to sleep.

Marcia was eleven years old when her family moved
from Maine to Lombard, Illinois, when she started playing the violin. Her father had been as excited about it as
she. Bert could still hear then, her first scratches and
scales, and he often sat at the piano accompanying her
meager tones. He graciously praised her, in spite of the
squeaks and uneven strokes of her bow across the strings.
His encouragement and support motivated her toward

each accomplishment on the intricate instrument, including a sonorous vibrato.

As her skill on the violin progressed, Marcia and Bert played duets in their house on Charlotte Street. In the living room where the piano sat in the corner under four Currier & Ives' prints, they played "Humoresque." Their joy and laughter often lured the rest of the family into the living room, creating mayhem and lively entertainment on many evenings.

In time, the rental instruments from school seemed less adequate and Marcia dreamed of having her own violin in the proper size with a resonant and mellow tone. The summer before she began high school, her father realized that dream for her one day when he brought home a brown leather case from the music store. Marcia held her breath as she turned the lock on the case and flipped open the two gold latches. The treasure inside lay cradled in orange velvet. The light illuminated the violin's warm patina, reflecting her delighted smile. "He bought it 'on time,'" Marcia wrote in her letter. It was the only thing Bert had ever bought by making payments, but he bought it because he wanted her to have it. He could not have afforded it otherwise.

Bolstered by her dad's enthusiasm, Marcia's skill with the violin steadily advanced. Her orchestra teacher yelled, "Love your instrument. Make it sing." So inspired, she and her dad went to the Glenbard West High School in Glen Ellyn to hear Vladimir Horowitz play piano. They were overjoyed to sit only thirty feet away from the great master in concert.

"Dad's music filled our homes and filled our hearts," Marcia wrote.

"He played the piano for us and for friends at birthdays, Christmas, and Thanksgiving. He especially played for our mother every day of their lives. He played most beautifully for her as her life slipped away."

Through their stories and in their home, I could see the sunshine in the Riedel family and hear the beauty of their music. Bert no longer had to see the sun streaming down nor hear his music to know their essence.

Enjoying the Moment

Something awakened me. I rolled over in bed to look at the red digital time displayed in the dark. It was 3:15 a.m. and Jim was sleeping soundly next to me. I had three more hours to sleep, but my brain was already fully engaged thinking about Bert. I always seemed to do my best thinking during those hours when I should have been sleeping. My mind raced with ideas for lessons with the Riedels. The three of them were soaking up sign language like thirsty sponges. I marveled at how well they'd adapted in a very short time to their new form of communication. And Bert had so much more potential, I wanted to sprint against time.

I looked at the clock again. It was 3:45 a.m. In only a few hours, I'd have a lesson with Bert and then a couple of interpreting assignments. I hoped that Matthew would remember his dental appointment before he went to his high school soccer camp. More important, I needed to take the program packet for the Silent Weekend to the printer. I had coordinated these weekends of immersion into sign language four times before, and once again my committee was expecting more than one hundred participants. The program and the instructors promised to be fabulous, but there were only ten days left until the event and I was anxious to get everything behind me. I also needed to focus on Heather. Her youth gymnastics career had recently ended with her graduation from high school, and we needed to start organizing her things for college. In a few weeks I'd be driving her to Ft. Lewis College in Durango, six hours away.

The clock said 6:30 a.m. I must have fallen back to sleep. It was light, and Jim was already gone. I jumped out of bed and hurried to the shower. A new vibrancy enveloped me. As I drove down our winding mountain road to the highway, the greenery of the pine forest against the blue sky seemed especially beautiful. The Riedels' house was across the highway, ten minutes more up winding roads, through aspen meadows and past horse pastures. My thoughts turned to the family's upcoming trip to California. They had plans to attend a wedding for Bert's granddaughter Alison. The garden wedding was to be at Marcia's home overlooking the San Francisco Bay. All the relatives would be there. This would be the first family gathering since Bert had moved away to Colorado and their first opportunity to see if sign language had made a difference in Bert's ability to interact.

In our lesson that morning we practiced some sign vocabulary for their trip: *airplane, train, California, wedding, vows,* and *family.* We made up name signs for various family members so John and Mary would be able to identify for Bert who he was talking to. Bert used me to rehearse the poem he was preparing to recite as a toast to the couple. Amid his thoughts of the joyous occasion, he remembered that Helen would not be there with him. "Do you think I should say something in honor of Helen at the wedding?" he asked me.

"Everyone knows you loved Helen," I said. "They loved her, too. I think you should keep the focus on the bride and groom at their wedding. You can talk about Helen afterward."

"I think you're right," he said. Bert was looking forward to the wedding—and so was I, even though I wouldn't be there. I felt confident it would be a positive and enjoyable experience for the Riedels. The tension around the communication problem was much less threatening now.

It was more than two weeks until I saw the family again. I couldn't wait to hear every detail about the wedding. "It was great," Mary said, bubbling forth a report. I listened, enthralled, about how they used their five months' worth of sign lessons to convey to Bert what was going on. Acting as amateur interpreters, John and Mary were able to engage him in simple conversations with others. We considered that a real feat, considering the circumstances of the previous twenty-five years.

"He got to enjoy the people and the wedding in the moment," Mary said. "He didn't have to wait days or weeks until we had time to type out a description of the whole event for him." Previously, Bert had sat silently through most family gatherings with a sad smile on his face. It was only an illusion that he was a participant. He'd been feigning enjoyment during those occasions. This time everyone was amazed at his transformation. He nearly stole the show from the bride and groom.

At the reception, Bert greeted and chatted with guests while Mary interpreted into his hand. After dinner the crowd became silent when John announced that his father had a special toast for the couple. They watched as John cued him when it was time to speak. Bert stood. Maintaining his touch to the chair, he walked around it to the back, where he placed his hands on the rim of its warm wood, keeping his balance. He was never comfortable standing alone in space without touching something. The contact helped him feel grounded. With all eyes on Bert, he began reciting the poem he'd composed.

The wedding of my granddaughter Alison is a
  pleasure for all,
A beautiful bride, fair and tall.
In a garden created with love of natural
  wonders,
Where my soul mate rests in peace.
With love from us here and those beyond,
This union of Ali and Blake is blessed with a
  heavenly bond.

"There was not a dry eye in that room," Mary said.

Trapped

As the fall months unfolded, opportunities expanded for Bert. His weekly schedule was filled with productive activity. His health had returned to near perfect, and our sign language lessons were moving ahead. All of us were happy. Then Mary had another idea.

"Diane," she said, "how would you like to teach Dad to type on a computer?"

"Why?" I asked, a little surprised.

"Because his old typewriter is worn out. The ribbon's bad and he can't see the mistakes. We thought since the computer has a spell-check function, it would save us from having to retype everything." She showed me a page he had typed recently. Some words ran together and some letters were ink-bare, but the writing was still legible.

"You do need a new ribbon," I agreed. I loved Bert's typing, with all of its imperfections. It was straight from his heart. I told Mary I'd think about the computer lessons. Soon after, however, came a major turn of events. On September 24, I'd just finished an interpreting assignment when my cell phone rang. It was John.

"Dad's in the hospital."

I felt my heart rise up and suddenly drop. "What happened?"

"He fell down the stairs yesterday. He fractured a vertebra in his neck."

I lost my breath for a minute and my heart started racing. Having worked at a spinal cord injury hospital during an internship in college, I'd seen many people paralyzed from accidents that had severed their spinal cords. I feared this had happened to Bert. "Is he paralyzed?"

I found out that Bert had been searching around the house for some braille Christmas poems written by Helen. After feeling through several boxes, he couldn't find them. He backtracked through his mind, trying to remember where he'd put them. A dreaded fear that someone had moved them or taken them or, worse, thrown them away, rushed through him. The poems were part of the few tangible remembrances he had of his beloved Helen. He had to find them. Carefully he made his way up the stairs, counting each step on the ascent. On the main floor he ran his fingers over each piece of furniture, scouring the rooms. The poems weren't there. He thought he must have missed them in the boxes downstairs. Obsessed with finding them, he decided to go back down and look again.

He felt for the door opening to the staircase with his cane. Normally, Bert took extra care to feel and count each step as he slid his hand down the rail. This time, his mind was elsewhere. In his angst, he misjudged his footing on one of the steps. His foot slipped and before he could catch himself by the handrail, he was tumbling down the stairs, falling six feet to the landing. John and Mary heard the awful bumping and banging and rushed from their downstairs office to see what had happened. They found him lying in a heap at the bottom of the stairs, groaning.

"Don't let him move," Mary commanded as she ran to call for emergency assistance. John attended to him and kept him immobile. The mountain-area response team arrived within fifteen minutes and determined that Bert might have a broken neck. Mary held onto Bert's hand. "STOP," she signed emphatically. It was the only sign she knew how to use at that moment. She signed it again.

"Oh, you don't want me to move," he said. He moaned with the pain while he complied with Mary's order. He lay still for the paramedics who transferred him onto the board so they could maneuver him up the same stairs he had just plummeted down. They put him into the ambulance and sped off to Swedish Hospital, forty miles away.

Mary stood at Bert's side in the emergency room, spelling words into his hands as the doctors determined he had sustained a dangerous fracture of the first cervical vertebra. If he had moved his head he could have severed the nerves that control his breathing. Fortunately, Mary had thought to communicate the critical word *stop* to him. Her quick action averted what could have been a worse disaster. Bert wasn't paralyzed, but he had to be heavily sedated for three days so that he wouldn't move while we waited for a halo—the metal head frame that would immobilize his neck. One in his size had to be flown in.

Those days were agonizingly long for me as I watched Bert lying in his hospital bed, inactive and nearly unconscious. His face was gray. His prominent cheekbones accentuated his sunken cheeks. His left wrist was broken and his hand was totally black and blue. The person lying there was not the vibrant man we all knew. I feared he'd get pneumonia and maybe die if he wasn't able to get up and move around soon.

I tried to rouse him and gingerly fingerspelled into his injured hand because that was the one he used most to read sign language. I held back tears as his fingers strained to read mine. The morphine confused him and my words were just muddle. He didn't know who I was.

The halo arrived, fortunately, before any pneumonia set in. The next time I saw Bert, eight days after the accident, he was sitting up in a chair with the halo screwed into four places in his head. He looked disheveled, unshaven, and uncomfortable with the heavy metal structure encircling his head. He had that unclean sour smell about him that reminded me of why I had felt so uncomfortable around elderly folks in my youth. The four vertical rods of the halo extended downward into a harness that enveloped his chest, almost to his waist. The halo held his head and neck in one position. He was to wear the halo for several months until the fracture healed. This time he recognized me, and he read a little fingerspelling. But the morphine was still too strong for him to really focus on the words.

"Diane, you are so kind to come here. I know it's a long way for you. This thing is a pain in the neck," he said, with a little laugh at his own joke. He pulled himself forward a bit. "Ohhhhh." His face scrunched with the look of pain. "I'm okay," he said, and leaned back in his chair. He seemed exhausted. I reached for the open can of chocolate Ensure from his bedside table and offered it to him. He took a sip from the straw. "Thank you, dear," he said, and pushed it back to me. I was worried about him, but even in his drugged state, his humor and lively spirit shined through. I knew he would get through this.

Mary had contacted all the people in Bert's community to let them know about his accident. Carrie, his neighbor from Conifer, stopped by the hospital on her way home from work. She told me about her visit.

"I was shocked," she said. "When I first walked in and saw him, I thought I had the wrong room. He looked so different with those screws in his head. It was almost too much to bear." She'd seen the power brailler on the table next to the bed. It now accompanied Bert wherever he went. John and Mary had brought it to the hospital so the staff would be able to communicate with him. Carrie hoped they were using it so that Bert would know what was going on, like when they were giving him medicine or taking him for X-rays. She noticed that Mary had posted signs on the wall above his bed instructing anyone who came into his room to announce themselves by typing their name into the laptop computer, then to direct Bert's hand onto the machine. Another sign read, "One tap anywhere means *no* and two taps means *yes.*"

Carrie moved over to the machine and typed, *hello Bert, this is Carrie, how are you doing?* She nudged his arm to let him know she was there.

"Who is it?" he asked in a weak voice. Automatically, he reached for the machine with his right hand. Luckily, his braille-reading hand was uninjured in the fall. His fingers felt for the dots. "Oh, Carrie, nice to see you. I took a tumble down the stairs and broke my neck. Mary told me not to move and the doctor says that saved my life! I have to wear this halo for three months. This is a pain in the neck," he said with a weak smile and a little chuckle. He repeated that joke to everyone. "I can't fix my hearing and I can't fix my vision, but I'm going to be the best patient you ever saw and I'm going to fix my neck."

Carrie and Bert chatted using the braille machine while Bert reported verbatim what the doctors and nurses had told him about his fracture. Carrie listened attentively for a half hour. "I have to go home now, Bert. I'm sure you'll be feeling better soon." The nurse walked in as Carrie turned to leave. "I'm a visitor," Carrie said. "I was just leaving."

"Isn't he delightful? Look at all he has to deal with," she commented, shaking her head. Carrie nodded and smiled.

Bert stayed in the hospital in the rehabilitation unit for nearly four weeks. Some of John and Mary's anxiety eased when the hospital arranged to have me there to interpret nearly every day between Bert and the doctors, nurses, and therapists. Bert had never used an interpreter before. He only knew me as his teacher, so he was confused about what I was doing there. He acted thrilled to see me anyway.

The interpreting took some creativity because Bert wasn't fluent enough to read sign language quickly. And the doctors didn't have the time to wait around until Bert understood all that they had to say. They were reluctant to use the braille machine and just wanted to tell me things and then leave. It gave Bert no opportunity to ask questions. I showed the therapists ways to communicate to him without talking. For Bert to do their exercise, they could move his arms or legs in the direction they wanted. Bert would imitate and repeat it. Or they could demonstrate the exercise on themselves while Bert felt the movement of their arm or leg. Bert was always cooperative and adept at copying.

I signed and spelled words in his now-splinted hand. The splint covered half of his hand and further hindered our communication. Just as in a courtroom when I asked the sheriff to remove a deaf inmate's handcuffs so that I could read the inmate's sign language, I asked the nurses, "Could we ask the doctor if it's possible to have the splint trimmed down, just a bit, so he could read my sign language?" The doctor's answer was *no*.

After the critical period was over, Bert was transferred to the Evergreen Life Care Center for further rehabilitation and twenty-four-hour care. The move meant another transition to new surroundings, with new people to meet.

John and Mary helped orient him to his new room by showing him the layout over and over again. Bert counted each step to the bathroom, each step to the sink, and each step back to the bed, memorizing where the furniture was placed so he wouldn't bump into it. When a new person entered his room at the hospital or at the Life Care Center, he asked them something about themselves. They typed their answer into the brailler and he committed it to memory. This was Bert's way. He found something remarkable about everyone. Even in his pain, he thought to thank each one who attended to him and made them feel like they were someone very special. "If you tell someone something nice and positive about them," he told me, "they will believe it. They will respond in a way that helps them to be a better person."

Despite Bert's positive outlook, the trauma to his body and the disruption of his life had me worrying about his long-term physical and mental health. I was also concerned that without his family around every day to reinforce the sign language, he might forget all that we had worked so hard for. His immediate challenges were learning to walk with a heavy metal halo screwed into his scalp, trying to sleep in a confined position in an unfamiliar bed, and getting used to institutional-style meals. He was struggling to get his strength back. Sign language instruction was the last thing on his mind. Fortunately, John and Mary believed it was essential to keep up his lessons while he was in rehabilitation, so I continued to see Bert regularly at the Life Care Center. I was someone consistent in his dark midst of nurses, doctors, and therapists.

The benefits of Bert's physical therapy would soon become evident. Twice a day, he imitated the motions demonstrated by his therapists. Relishing their attention and the exercise, he quickly regained his energy and the hand splint came off, too. I was greatly relieved to see these transitions. When I arrived, I loved seeing his face light up and his body shimmer with glee when I spelled my name into his hand. That alone was a gift that made the visits worthwhile for me. Trapped in a halo, without sight or hearing, he still radiated enthusiasm while telling me about what he'd been thinking or reading. He provided details about conversations he shared with people he was meeting there. Sometimes, though, his mood was not so positive and cheerful. About a month into his convalescence he disclosed his frustrations.

"It's not easy trying to fit into a sighted and hearing world," he admitted. "They take me to the dining room and seat me at a table with other people. I don't know who's there, who I'm sitting with, so I can't even make polite conversation. It's uncomfortable to wait for an interminable length of time after dinner for an aide to take me back to my room. I wave my hand in the air wondering, is anyone there? Can they see me? What are they doing? Do they see that I'm finished eating?"

Without the braille machine in the dining room, no one was able to communicate with Bert. It was painful for him and for me that he had to deal with people who were insensitive or undereducated about his plight. Sometimes Bert asked me questions about something someone did or said that he didn't quite understand or that confused him. He wanted to know more but was embarrassed to ask them too many questions. People often didn't take the time to explain everything to him. They didn't understand that he was missing out on so much important information. They didn't know what it felt like to be trapped in darkness and silence.

CHAPTER TWELVE

Barriers of Deafness

Because a hearing deficiency isn't visible, it's not obvious to the rest of the world that deaf people don't pick up the wealth of information around them —information that hearing people take in effortlessly from the radio, TV, and from incidental conversations. Bert was missing out on all of these. Without his sight, he was also denied the visual information the rest of us absorb without realizing it.

When a deaf-blind person like Bert looks normal and speaks normally because he learned language before he lost his hearing, it's easy to forget that he's not like everyone else. The care center staff and I needed to be sensitive to Bert's barriers. We needed to take extra time to communicate the things he was missing. I was especially sensitive to the barriers because I confronted them every day in my interpreting work. Breaking them down was always challenging, but some days were even more so than others—like when I interpreted for individuals with minimal language.

Because these individuals have been deprived of education, formal sign language is ineffective with them. My skills are tested in a different way with this group (twenty-five percent of the deaf population)[14] because I have to depend mostly on gestures, mime, and drawing pictures. The circumstances are akin to trying to communicate with someone who doesn't speak your language. If you're trying to get that person to do something, you simply demonstrate the action and motion for them to imitate. If you're trying to elicit information, the task becomes more complicated. It requires an amazing amount of mental and physical energy.

I enjoy doing this kind of work; however, it is good to team with relay interpreters, or CDIs (certified deaf interpreters), as we now call them, because they are more adept than I am at using gestures and mime. They enhance what I—a hearing interpreter—can do alone. And interesting things happen during the task of breaking down the barriers. One day, something occurred that made me realize just how far the invisible barriers reach. I am highly tuned into them, but this one, unrelated to deafness, almost got past me.

I had arrived early to the courthouse to get acquainted with the deaf man and the CDI I'd be working with. At seven-thirty in the morning, the halls of the courthouse were sparsely populated and I was the first one on our case to show up. I sat down to wait, and after about five minutes two Hispanic men walked past me. Since I didn't know the person I was waiting for, I studied the men to see if they'd start signing. They didn't. They didn't talk to each other either. They stopped in front of the courtroom and looked at the list of names on the docket. I watched them shake their heads and move on to the next courtroom where another docket was posted. One of the men wore a clean white T-shirt. When I saw him motion something to the other, I thought both men were deaf. They turned at the end of the hall and started walking back toward me.

When the man in the white T-shirt made eye contact with me, I signed to him while simultaneously speaking,

"You deaf?" They both stopped walking and looked at me. The one in the white shirt motioned again, pointing to his ear and then to the taller man next to him. It was clear by this time that one or both of them were deaf, but I couldn't tell which. The taller one stood stiffly, regarding me without expression. The one motioning was more animated, though I couldn't understand his gestures. I didn't know if he meant that he himself was deaf or that the expressionless man was. In my puzzlement, I recognized a communication barrier but couldn't identify what kind it was.

I stood and asked them while signing, "Do you know sign language?" Again, the one in the white shirt only gestured. Then the taller man handed me a piece of paper. It was a summons bearing a name I didn't recognize. A room number designated a courtroom two floors up. I spoke the name and signed, "No, you're not with me." I gestured between us, waving my hands back and forth. "You upstairs," I pointed. "I'm waiting for someone else."

I handed him back his paper. He resumed his stiff stare. The expressive one gestured for the man to go upstairs. Suddenly, I understood. The one in the white T-shirt was indeed deaf, and the taller man could hear but didn't speak English. I tested my assumption by using my rusty and awkward Spanish. "Hablas español?"

A little smile broke from his stiffness. "Si."

The man in the white T-shirt didn't speak at all. I figured then that *he* was the person I was waiting for and I said to the Spanish-speaking man, "Esta lugar, no esta aqui," pointing to his summons, indicating he was in the wrong place. "Tú necesitas ir arriba." You need to go upstairs.

"Arriba?" he asked.

"Si."

"Gracias." He thanked me and left us in the hallway. The deaf man showed me some court papers he'd pulled from his pocket. The name confirmed he was the person I was waiting for. Since the CDI hadn't yet arrived and the interpreting agency had informed me that our client had minimal language, I was mindful to use gestures and not actual signs. "Yes," I nodded, and pointed to us, "you and I."

It became clear that the two men had encountered one another in the hallway when the Spanish-speaking man asked this minimal-language deaf fellow for directions. Just as the confusion resolved, my teammate joined us. We tried conversing with our client before starting our work in the courtroom. She wanted to know how long he had worked for Tony's Pizza. She figured he worked there from his T-shirt advertising the pizza parlor. The question turned into a ten-minute pantomime between them. She pointed to him and acted out kneading and pulling pizza dough, sliding pizza in and out of an oven, and then pointed to the words on his shirt. With her index finger she outlined numbers on her palm—1998 and 1999, followed by a display of her hands, with palms up. A questioning facial expression accompanied her hand gesture. He responded by outlining numbers with his finger on the smooth wood of the bench we were sitting on— the years corresponding to his employment.

Her next question, "Do you work there regularly or now and then?" necessitated a lot more miming of kneading pizza dough, sleeping, kneading, sleeping, and kneading. She pointed to many days on the calendar inside my appointment book and ran her finger across several of the weeks. Again, she wore the same questioning facial expression. He eagerly responded to her inquiry by pointing to some of the days on the calendar with a side-to-side shake of his head. After all of that, we still weren't sure we understood his answer to her question.

In the courtroom, the questions from the city attorney took an equal amount of time to convey and to elicit his responses. With great patience, the attorney allowed the CDI and me to take all the time we needed to ensure that the deaf citizen had adequate communication, affording him all of his rights under the law. After a half hour with this one defendant on her morning's full docket, the attorney sighed and finally said, "Let's set this case over for a day with the public defender." We left the busy courthouse and I did not see the gesturing deaf man again.

It is often like that—where we never see clients again, or for long periods of time. There is not always follow-through or consistency with assignments. Moreover, because interpreters follow a code of confidentiality, we do not discuss cases with each other. As a result, I am often left wondering how events turned out for the deaf clients. Did the public defender resolve the case for the gesturing man, or did the judge simply throw the case out? Barriers of deafness are often too complicated to overcome in the fast pace of our hearing world.

Is It Snowing Outside?

Bert had major advantages over people with minimal language because he acquired language before losing his hearing. He didn't suffer the same consequences from the language barrier as those born deaf who often wrestle with English. He was able to read, and he received the *New York Times* in braille. Unlike people with minimal language, Bert was informed of what was going on in the world. Yet he experienced other, more immediate, barriers. He got his *New York Times* two weeks later than everyone else got their newspapers. And he had no access to local news, no way of knowing what was happening in his own town or right outside his door. Unlike someone with the single handicap of deafness, Bert couldn't look out a window to see what the weather was doing. "Is it snowing outside?" he would ask. "Without the sun's warmth on my skin, I can't even tell if it's day or night." Most people didn't think to tell Bert these seemingly little things, like delivery men who neglected to inform Bert when they dropped off gifts and cards for him at the Life Care Center. One Saturday, I found an unopened greeting card on the table. I wondered if Bert knew it was there. I put it in his hand. He felt the familiar shape.

"Is this a card? Who is it from?" he asked. He opened it and I saw the name.

"From D-a-w-n," I signed. She was a friend of mine who knew sign language and sometimes accompanied me to Bert's house. I took his finger and used it to outline the drawing of the heart with a smiling face on the front of the card. It took him several times to get what I was doing. "It's a heart," he finally said. "What does it say?"

I proceeded to sign the message inside, knowing it would take a while to convey it to him this way. I was resolute to see that Bert use sign language and I unfalteringly avoided using the braille machine. "I came here—"

"I bring," he said.

"No, c-a-m-e," I spelled. "I came here."

"Oh, I see. I came. I came yesterday," he guessed.

"No, here, h-e-r-e, here." I signed it, spelled it, and signed it again with both of my index fingers pointing down to the ground in front of me.

"I came *here*," he interpreted correctly.

"Yes," I tapped twice on his knee. "To visit you."

"To . . . uh . . . now, what is that word?"

"Visit," I signed.

He still didn't get it. I spelled it. He slowly read each letter out loud, "V, i, b. No, not b; s . . . i . . . n. What is visin?"

I made the sign again, *visit*. I put his hands into the letter *v* handshapes and helped him make the sign. Then I spelled the word again into his hand: v-i-s-i-t.

"Visit," he said at last.

Although the process was laborious, Bert stayed with me. We continued in the same manner until we got through the entire note: ". . . but you were asleep. You give such joy to so many. I hope you get well soon, Bert. I miss you. Love, Dawn."

He got the message, finally. It took us almost twenty minutes. We each sat back in our chair. Tears filled his eyes.

We had accomplished something good for that day. Both of us were a little tired by this point, so I gave in to my resolution never to use the braille machine. I used it at the end of our lesson to encourage Bert to get over his fear of being impolite and to speak up and ask for what he needed. It made me think about the piano I had seen down the hall, in the activity room, and how much Bert loved to play.

"Do you know there is a piano here?" I asked. He didn't know. "Be assertive," I typed. "Tell them you want to go play the piano, and don't wait for someone to ask you. They are very busy. They won't think to ask you."

"I don't want to be bothering them," he said.

"You're not bothering them. That's their job, and they're happy to do it. You need to ask questions. People won't look down on you for that—they'll look up to you. They need to know when they haven't communicated effectively with you." I emphasized that he didn't need to pretend he was understanding things when he wasn't. He was responsible for letting others know what he wanted or needed.

"That sounds pretty simple, doesn't it?" he said. "You think of everything. You're my advocate."

"Will you play the piano for me now?"

"Yes, I can do that," he said, and smiled.

I'd never known Bert to turn down any suggestion or invitation. He was always up for anything, even on the spur of the moment. He pushed himself up from his chair and, with a few grunts and groans, felt for his cane. I handed it to him. "Thank you," he said, as usual.

I led him down the hallway toward the activity room. Residents seated in wheelchairs turned their heads to watch us as we ambled by. Those who could speak tried to say something to Bert. Others, simply by their expressions, showed their awe for the deaf and blind man with the halo on his head who chatted cheerfully as we passed them. I knew Bert was oblivious to their presence and to their reactions to him. He was perhaps a few years older than most of them, yet he was more sprite and alert, seemingly years younger.

A small group of elderly women, most of whom were in wheelchairs, occupied the activity room that day. One woman was so severely disabled that she looked comatose and stiff, her muscles contracted from long-term disuse. No one spoke as I guided Bert's hand onto the piano bench. He maneuvered himself onto the seat. His fingers expertly oriented themselves to the piano keys, and he began to play Beethoven's "Pathetique." The aides wheeled in a few more residents to listen to the music. The room filled with life. Bert transitioned into the old Irish song "Danny Boy," striking a chord of familiarity with a couple of the residents. I suspected they hadn't spoken much in months, but the song suddenly flowed out from them in voices retrieved from their youth. This time tears came to *my* eyes. Bert was unaware there was anyone in the room besides the two of us. When he finished the piece I signed to him, "The women are singing."

"They are?" he exclaimed. "How many are there?"

"Ten."

Pure pleasure crossed his face. "I'm glad they liked it." He continued playing, first Mendelssohn's "Wedding March" and then Dvorak's *New World Symphony*.

• • • • •

I was honored and flattered that Bert saw me as his advocate; however, I hadn't lost sight that I was his sign language teacher. My goal was to facilitate his and the

Riedels' learning to the point where they could communicate comfortably in sign language.

Because I believe that the best way to learn sign is to use it, I concentrated on using manual communication as much as possible and avoided falling back on the easy way to talk, using the braille machine. The more exposure Bert had to sign language, the more probability he would incorporate it into his life. Working together only three hours a week over the three months Bert would spend at the Life Care Center, we had a mountain to climb. There was virtually no one else there who could sign to him. Neither could his family be with him daily to bolster his progress. It was frustrating for me as well as for Bert. He would often stumble on forgotten signs he had once known and would scold himself for not being more proficient. I pushed, just to get him to maintain the basic level of skill he had achieved. It was a contest for me because I knew Bert was content to do all the talking. Talking was easier than doing the work required to decipher the language I was feeding him—literally by hand.

As fascinated as I was by what he had to say, I was more strongly driven to have Bert absorb the value of the gift I held for him. My job was to find creative ways to integrate sign language into our conversations, to make it meaningful and interesting for him. I strove to keep exposing signs to him, bit by bit, until he finally grasped the gravity of their usefulness. Up until this time, it seemed that Bert thought sign language was merely a fun game between us. Still I believed the time would come when he would fully understand its true value. A broken neck and wrist were just temporary roadblocks on his journey.

Friends

As Bert's stay at the Life Care Center lengthened into October, the community of people in his life began growing little by little. Peggy Grant, a mother of three grown children, came in as a volunteer and soon became one of his regular companions. Bert often spoke of Peggy and how he enjoyed his lengthy talks and card games with her. When I finally met her, she described her first encounter with Bert.

"When I walked into his room, I was surprised by the array of equipment there. You don't normally find that kind of stuff in a nursing facility," she said. "There was an exercise bicycle, stacks of papers and hard-bound volumes, and two weird-looking machines on a table." Peggy couldn't guess what the large hard-bound volumes were, nor the thick magazines full of plain brown pages. They were piled on the spare bed and on top of two dressers. She didn't notice the nearly imperceptible little bumps on their stiff pages until she saw the large black words printed across the top of the title page: "The National Geographic." Similar to those magazines were others with white pages titled, "The New York Times."

Stretched out on the bed was Bert, who she described as "dashingly handsome, with his shock of pure white hair." He was dressed and fully awake, staring out into space with his powder blue eyes. He looked oddly sophisticated, lying with his head elevated from the bed by the halo of metal. Peggy stood still for a moment, making some mental assessments before she approached him and introduced herself as a volunteer. But there was no response from Bert.

"I didn't understand this," Peggy told me, "because this was the way I always greeted the residents when I first met them." Confused, she placed her hand lightly on Bert's shoulder and repeated a little louder, "Hi, I'm Peggy Grant."

Bert startled at her touch, sat up quickly, and encircled her hand with his. "Hellooo," he said in his singsong voice. His eyes stared straight ahead. She tried to converse with him further, raising her voice louder so that he could hear her. He still didn't respond.

"Could you tell me your name on the machine?" he asked.

It was clear to her now that he was blind and couldn't hear either. Moving over to the brailler, Peggy clumsily typed out her name on the laptop computer and reiterated that she was a volunteer. Bert slowly made his way to the machine. Peggy watched him follow the raised dots on the power brailler with his index finger. She remained at the machine while Bert interpreted the words aloud.

"Peggy, it's nice to meet you. You're a volunteer? What do you do here?"

Enchanted by his immediate interest in her, along with his unusual communication equipment, Peggy slid down into the chair next to the brailler, engaged into his conversation. Bert began describing the circumstances of his limitations due to Usher Syndrome and the nasty fall he had taken down the stairs. He didn't omit the details of having recently lost his wife and his subsequent move to Colorado. His expression changed when he spoke of Helen.

His face reddened and his words trailed off into a whisper. At the end of his short biographical sketch, Bert turned his attention to Peggy. "How did you come to be a volunteer here, Peggy?"

"I've been spending Monday afternoons here as a friendly visitor since 1991," she typed. "I just like to be with the people here." Peggy had shared in the lives of many residents, with the mission of being an empathetic listener, helping to relieve the suffering of chronic loneliness. Over the years, she had heard stories of hardship, illness, depression, and sadness, but Bert's story was different. He shared factual information, leaving out the self-pity that some other nursing home residents expressed.

Peggy visited Bert frequently after their first meeting. Their talks spanned a range of topics such as evolution, politics, economics, the stock market, nature, music, or one of Bert's favorites, the philosophy of life. From time to time Bert delved into the realities of his current situation—the halo that was keeping him from the freedom he had enjoyed at Mary and John's home. His eyes still welled up when his sentiments drifted to Helen. He admitted to Peggy that sometimes he felt the tug of negativity and did feel sorry for himself.

"How do you get your positive attitude back?" Peggy wanted to know. His face turned serious. "Whenever I start to feel sorry for myself, I think about all I have to be grateful for and about the people in the world who have less than I do. I've had a wonderful life, and I have a remarkable family." Bert's mood lightened and he changed the subject to talk about some "interesting person" he had met that day.

Awakening

FUGUE

I sought to find a song to lift my heart
Out of the doldrums of the commonplace:
* A melody that I could keep apart*
And call my own, defying time and space.
A song to match all seasons of the soul,
Forged from the best of all life's harmonies;
a perfect rhythm keyed to every goal,
a shield of hope against uncertainties.
But none of all the tempos that I tried
seemed adequate to hold the shifting themes
that rose and fell, a great discordant tide
of stark realities and hopeful dreams.
Instead I let life's music rise and fall;
I laughed and loved and cried and that
* was all.*

—Robert J. Smithdas

In the summer months before Bert broke his neck, he frequently talked about Robert Smithdas, the director of community education at the Helen Keller National Center in Sands Point, New York. Smithdas was the first deaf-blind person to have earned a master's degree in the United States from New York University in 1952. He was the editor of the center's magazine, *Nat-Cent News*.

Bert occasionally submitted articles that were published in the magazine.

"I was curious to know more about this man," Bert said during one of those summer lessons. "So I spent some time tracking down a brailled copy of his autobiography, *Life at My Fingertips*." Bert learned that Smithdas had lost his eyesight at age four and a half from spinal meningitis but still had some hearing until about age ten. "At that point in his life, he was the same as I was in my early eighties. It took me fifty years to get to the degree of loss he had at age ten."

Bert was so impressed with this blind child, he couldn't stop talking about him. "Bobby had a profound hunger for knowing what things looked like. Desperately he applied his fingertips to everything in sight, one might say. After he memorized all the physical details inside his home, he went outdoors and examined his mother's garden. From there he explored the whole neighborhood, including cracks in the sidewalk and slants in the pavement. He used the scents of trees and shapes of hedges to identify the homes on his route. Then when he was six years old, Bobby was sent to a school for the blind."

As usual I held Bert's hand as he talked, aware that he was relating to Robert Smithdas in a way he had related to no one else. Soon I had become curious about this man, too. When I began to sign a question to Bert, he paused for a moment feeling my hand movements. But he was so absorbed he let my question sail off into the air. He kept on talking, telling me about the boys who called Bobby "Smearcase."

"The other boys were only blind, not deaf," Bert said. "Bobby was the only deaf-blind student. They made fun of him and called him Smearcase because he handled and smelled everything he touched. They shoved him from behind and ran away when he crashed to the ground. In anger he got up and tore after them, only to end up colliding with the wall." Bert moved forward and back and from side to side as he spoke. He shook his head and his eyes teared. "I remember how cruel kids used to tease me for my clumsiness," he said, recollecting his own childhood. "They didn't know it was caused by my vision and hearing problems."

As Bert had survived the childhood hazing, so did Robert Smithdas. In spite of it, he had done well in school, and his teachers encouraged him to apply to the university.

Bert continued. "Just as Smithdas was starting college, he got to meet Helen Keller. She was sixty-five years old then and they spoke by fingerspelling into each other's hands. She had graduated fifty years before from Radcliff College. She told him she was confident he would succeed in college, too." Bert explained that Smithdas had a companion at the university who sat beside him during lectures to transmit the information through fingerspelling. With his drive, Robert Smithdas graduated cum laude and later obtained a master's degree.

Bert spoke passionately about Smithdas's accomplishments. It was unimaginable to him that someone could grasp an understanding of his world through just his fingertips. I wanted to read Bert's book, but I couldn't read braille. I felt handicapped and left out of the discussion each time he brought up the subject. Finally, near the end of October, I discovered Bob Smithdas myself. My daughter, Heather, called me to the television as Barbara Walters was interviewing him on *20/20*. I couldn't wait to tell Bert what I'd seen. It was several days later when I got the chance.

Bert sat stiffly under his halo while I faced him in my chair. "I want tell you who I d-i-d see on TV," I signed. "It was R-o-b-e-r-t, S-m-i-t-h-d-a-s. He has wife. H-e-r name is M-i-c-h-e-l-l-e."

Bert was surprised and interested. He wanted to know what Michelle looked like. "She is small. Her hair is d-a-r-k and s-h-o-r-t," I showed him with my fingertips lining my chin. He wanted to know if she was also deaf-blind. "She is blind," I told him, and then explained by typing into the braille machine that she was deaf but acquired some hearing since receiving a cochlear implant.

Barbara Walters described Bob Smithdas as "a teacher and a poet and the most memorable person she had ever met." The program depicted how the Smithdases lived independently, cooking by touch and using pagers to receive signals from the Teletype (telephone) or the door-bell, or to locate each other in the house.

I pictured a friendship between Bert and Robert Smithdas. "You can write him l-e-t-t-e-r," I suggested. "He will love to hear from you." Bert wondered if Smithdas would share the same fascination he had with paleontol-ogy, which had been his focus since reading the latest *National Geographic*. For several weeks, Bert pondered writing to Smithdas and created several versions of a letter, mentioning that one of his interests included pale-ontology. Finally, Bert settled on one letter that he felt was worthy and sent it.

While anticipating the reply, he remained absorbed in reading Smithdas's poetry until he almost forgot about his own misery in the ever-present halo. This literally heavy burden was interfering with the living he still had left to do.

"All through my life I've met major challenges result-ing from my dwindling eyesight and hearing." Bert said.

"Now I'm trapped in a halo and I'm further denied the many things I want to do. Since I started to reflect on these incredible poems, written by a deaf-blind man, I felt guilty. I was lucky compared to him. I realized I had to rediscover the value of human relationships. I want to be in constant contact with people who understand my limitations from now on."

Bert had experienced an awakening. He realized that over time he had resigned himself to living in a dark silent world—a world that did not understand deafness. A world without friends. Now he saw it did not have to be so dark and lonely. When hands could speak to hands, body language full of emotion and expression flowed directly to him. He was reconnected to the human race. He would never need to fear being severed by Usher Syndrome.

With a renewed sense of hope and possibility Bert continued his wait for a response from Robert Smithdas. As the wait grew longer, we spoke of him less and less, yet, I knew the impact of Smithdas remained strong because Bert began studying sign language in earnest. We moved on. In due course, we heard from Smithdas and I was pleased.

CHAPTER SIXTEEN

Simple Exchange

Bert pushed through the fall months with his physical rehabilitation and our sign language lessons. Twice he overcame painful infections at the pin sites where the halo was screwed into his skull. Now, as the first day of winter approached, Bert had regained his strength and was eager to go home. We were just waiting to find out if the fracture had healed. If so, the halo would come off and Bert would be released.

It was pleasant and sunny when I pulled into the parking lot of the Life Care Center. The well-kept building nestled against the foothills outlined by a sharp blue sky. I grabbed my bag from the backseat and jumped out of the car. The brisk air felt light and clean against my face. Inside, the receptionist greeted me.

"Hello," I said, but didn't stop to chat. Typically I walked fast, but today I quickened my steps to Bert's room, hoping to hear good news about him going home. The halls were clear of the distasteful odors I sometimes detected in nursing homes. Instead, there were aromas of meatloaf and peas coming from the dining room. As I walked past the activity room, I heard the sounds of a bingo game. "B-13" rang from a strong feminine voice. I thought it was sad that Bert couldn't join in group activities, but I doubted whether he'd find bingo very stimulating anyway.

Usually Bert was lying on top of his bedspread reading his braille magazines when I arrived. This time he was sitting on the bed's edge, engaged in an animated discussion with Shannon, a nurse's aide. She was a small, dark-haired high school student. Shannon had aspirations of going to medical school, and Bert, always impressed with ambition, was inquiring about her future plans. I stood back, observing their simple exchange as she tapped on his hand her "yes" and "no" answers to his questions.

Bert and Shannon were having a swell time. The conversation flowed as Bert talked and asked questions and Shannon tapped. A calm realization rippled through me. For months, Bert had seemed resistant to incorporating the hand signs for *yes* and *no*. Usually he confused *no* with the signs for *a little bit* or *twenty. Yes,* an up-and-down shake of the closed fist, seemed to escape him entirely. But there was no confusion with Shannon. Communication was the point—not the method but the act itself. Although tapping was not a part of formal sign language, and I had considered it barbaric, I saw it was quite effective here. Why should I make him fix something that didn't need fixing? If Bert was comfortable with the taps for *yes* and *no*, then that was what we'd use.

When Shannon stood to leave, I stepped forward to take Bert's hand. He noticed I was someone different. "Who is this?" he asked.

"D-i—"

"Oh, Diane," he said, before I finished spelling my name. "Nice to see you." He jumped right in to answer my question before I even asked it. "The doctor gave me his report." Bert's brow furrowed and the sparkle in his eyes changed to a disquieting stare. "The fracture's not quite healed, and he thinks it will take three more weeks."

My heart sank. We were silent for a moment. "The doctor knows what's best for me. I'll just have to accept it," he said, shrugging his shoulders. We both looked for something to say to comfort each other. "I can be patient, and soon enough I'll be able to go home," he added resolutely. I knew he was covering up his disappointment with a positive stance. Bert never wallowed in his misery.

Knowing he would be going home with the New Year, Bert changed his focus to one last thing he wanted to do before leaving the Life Care Center—to present a Christmas concert to the residents and staff he had grown fond of. During the next two weeks he busied himself with planning and rehearsing a medley of Christmas carols on the piano. He and John worked out the details of how he would be introduced and the method for cueing him between carols. Bert made certain everything was in order. He asked Mary to design a sign inviting everyone to attend, and he arranged for her to bring treats, poinsettias, and red candles to place on each side of the piano. The Life Care Center offered to provide the cookies and punch.

A few days before the concert, Bert was unable to concentrate on our sign language lesson. With nervous excitement, he kept talking about the concert. While I knew Bert was presenting a Christmas program on Tuesday afternoon, until now I had been unaware of the extent of his planning. He talked about the decorations and outlined the order of the carols he planned to play. He described how John would poke him gently in the ribs when it was time to begin playing.

I started thinking this event was going to be much larger than I'd originally thought—and it was taking precedence over our sign language lesson, so I dropped the lesson. I asked Bert, "How many people are coming to your

Bert in his "halo" has a one-way phone conversation with a friend.

concert?" I hadn't seen an invitation and didn't know how he had announced it.

"About two hundred."

Two hundred? Where, I wondered, was this concert going to be held? Had they rented a concert hall someplace? "Where will you have—"

"Right here," he said.

"Who will be coming?"

"The residents, the staff, and their families," he answered nonchalantly.

About forty people turned out for Bert's concert on Tuesday. He hadn't realized that many of the residents couldn't get out of their beds to join us. Some residents sat in their wheelchairs in rows; others took up the remaining chairs filling the room. Busy staff members dropped in and out as they could. Mary and I sat in the doorway, partly because there was no room for us inside, and also so I could watch for my husband, Jim. I had convinced him to take off early from work to come to this special event. It had been nine months since I started working with the Riedels and Jim had never met the people he'd heard so much about.

Bert wore his best red shirt, which accented his white hair and matched the candles and poinsettias decorating the room. The halo, obvious and heavy on his head, limited his movement but not his motivation. John opened the program by introducing his father and thanking everyone for coming. He passed out sheets with the words to the carols and urged everyone to sing along. When John nudged his father, Bert knew to begin. He started with "Joy to the World."

I was anxious that Jim hadn't arrived yet, worried he would miss Bert's concert. Halfway through the second song, "O Come All Ye Faithful," I was relieved when he showed up. Jim stood with Mary and me in the doorway, looking in with amazement at the deaf-blind pianist. As Bert played the traditional carols, we sang along unseen and unheard by him, though no doubt pictured clearly in his mind.

The performance wasn't that of a virtuoso, yet Bert's attitude reflected the choices he had made throughout his life. With vigor and passion, Bert chose not to remain paralyzed in depression but to embrace that which was good amidst formidable circumstances. He had given Christmas concerts all of his life. Why should being confined to a nursing home and a halo stop him now? Bert's spirit affected all of us in the room. I came away from his concert celebrating—forgetting my trivial problems and appreciating life a little more.

CHAPTER SEVENTEEN

Words in My Hands, Notes in My Heart

Words are the mind's wings, are they not?
—HELEN KELLER, age eleven
Letter to Oliver Wendell Holmes, May 27, 1891

The snow in January didn't daunt my Subaru wagon as it easily maneuvered our steep driveway. The dirt roads had been plowed, allowing commuters a nonstressful trip down the mountain. A small orange fox with a black-and-white-tipped tail hastened across the road in front of me. Heading down the highway on my usual route, I felt as though I lived in the city. Mostly, I lived in my car. The seats were filled with items that designated the various roles I assumed. Like a chameleon subtly changing colors, I slipped in and out of those roles.

A canvas bag stuffed with files and folders for my son's soccer team lay next to a backpack filled with notebooks and dictionaries for my Spanish class. Snow boots, tennis shoes, and changes of clothing mingled with an assortment of jackets for rain or snow. And there were books. Always books. The rear of the vehicle was reserved for carrying dogs, tools, and miscellaneous construction materials for Jim's business.

When I wasn't being Mom, the soccer team manager, or the construction gopher ("Go-Fer"), I was the sign language interpreter. I transported words like the courier who carries and delivers packages without delving into their contents. Like the money-changing machine that sucks up dollar bills and spits out quarters, my eyes took in signs and the words rolled off my tongue.

When I first began interpreting, I wondered at the end of an interpreting day what I "produced" for society. One male colleague said to me once about what he does:"I copy people—that's my job." But it's not always so nice and neat or as easy as that. We aren't machines. Sometimes there are no signs or words to convey thoughts exactly as they have been expressed from one language to another. It requires a lot of fast-brain work to come up with equivalents. And often, no matter how professional I remain on the outside, I'm stirring emotionally inside.

Today was no exception. Despite the overnight snowstorm, I arrived on time to my first assignment. After speaking with the clerk, I sat on one of the crowded benches in the courtroom. In the flurry of activity, I watched for the deaf client and listened for our case. The judge called it just as the deaf man entered the room. I motioned him to the lectern and took my place near the judge.

"What's this about women's clothing?" the judge asked, as he read from the case file. I stood interpreting his words into sign as the defendant and plaintiff, both deaf, looked on.

"He was wearing a dress!" the defendant signed.

"I have a right to wear whatever I want," the plaintiff retorted.

My voice gave spoken life to their signed words. I played out the scenario in the courtroom, holding my own surprised reaction behind a professional reserve. The plaintiff asked for reimbursement from the defendant for damages to his attire that ensued during an altercation between them.

"Are there any witnesses?" the judge asked. There were none. "Very well, then. I'm dismissing this case for insufficient evidence. You're all free to leave."

The wind brushed my face when I opened the door upon leaving the courthouse. I stepped cautiously down the steps and around the patches of ice on the freshly shoveled sidewalk. I zipped my jacket up under my chin in an ill attempt against the chill. Shivering, I walked back to my car.

There were more than four hours until I was to see Bert. I could do the errands Jim had for me: "Pick up the saw blades, drop off the nail gun for repairs, pick up the hardware, and drop off the sets of plans—one to the electrician and one to the plumber, as soon as you can. I love you. I'm late," he had said this morning on his way out the door. I didn't mind the errands, but sometimes I liked to read or go shopping in between my interpreting assignments.

When I got to the car, there was a message on my cell phone from the interpreting agency. They needed an interpreter at the hospital right away. "The deaf patient has AIDS," the coordinator informed me when I phoned her back. "The social worker needs an interpreter so she can talk to him."

"Okay, sure, I'll do it," I said. The saw blades and hardware could wait.

"Thank you for taking this, Diane. I'll call the social worker and tell her you're on your way."

I met up with the social worker in the hospital lobby. "I'm glad you could come on such short notice. Anthony has AIDS and I need to talk to him about preparations for his last weeks. This may not be easy," she warned me in the hallway leading up to his room.

We entered his room together. Anthony lay in bed, propped up with pillows. Several deaf friends stood near wearing tearful expressions. The social worker introduced us while I realized I already knew a couple of them. "We need to speak to Anthony," she told them. I interpreted. They nodded their heads and moved away from the bed. We moved closer to Anthony, who lay still except for brief, irregular gasps of air. His eyes were open, but they didn't connect with anything or anyone. The social worker began speaking but I didn't sign her words. As an interpreter I'm supposed to always sign everything that is spoken. In this case I recognized Anthony's agonal breathing and knew that the next intake of air might be his last.

"I don't think he's with us," I whispered.

"It's almost the end," his friend signed.

We stepped away from the bed. The long pauses between his gasps were difficult to witness. The social worker talked to his friends about wrapping up Anthony's final transactions. He had no family there. A few minutes later, Anthony took his last breath. The nurse came in and asked us if we wanted to stay a few more minutes with the body. I interpreted what she said to the friends. With red eyes, they motioned that they wanted to stay a while longer. I left with the social worker.

• • • • •

Each day of interpreting is an eye-opener to me of the human condition, which is compounded by the communication barrier of deafness. I am the channel between the doctors in the emergency room and a deaf woman who has attempted suicide. I am there when the same woman confesses later to her therapist that she hates her life. She says her family hadn't communicated with her while she was growing up. They didn't know how.

I express the judge's sentence to a deaf mother when he sends her teenage daughter to jail for failure to comply with the conditions of her probation. The girl had been ordered to attend school regularly after being convicted for hiding a gun in her purse. Instead, she dropped out. Behind my professional mask, I grieve for her mother when she collapses into tears in the courtroom.

I have to use profanity with another judge. As a deaf inmate is led out of the courtroom by the sheriff, the judge catches his emphatic signing. "Bring him back," the judge orders. "What did you say?" he demands from the defendant. My knees fall weak. I say the words out loud to the judge. "F——— you."

I cry through a deaf woman's vivid description of her mother's demise from cancer as I articulate her story to her therapist. Inside I am reliving my own experience. I have just lost my own mother.

Peering under a tent of surgical drapes, donned in sterile green scrubs, I break the surgeon's news to the deaf patient lying awake on the operating table: "Sorry, we made a terrible mistake. We cut open the wrong side."

With a lump in my throat, I speak for a deaf man asking the funeral home director if there are any other caskets, more moderately priced, in which to bury his beloved wife.

Another time, I am interpreting for a deaf mother in a conference for her son. The meeting with the teacher and the boy's therapist is already a half hour late in starting when blood starts pouring from my nose. They wait patiently fifteen minutes more for me, though the bleeding persists. "Would you mind going ahead with one hand?" the therapist asks. "We can't delay this meeting any longer."

"Sure, sorry about this," I say, and proceed to interpret with one hand while holding a tissue to my copious nosebleed. I give expression with one half of my face. The deaf mother tells me afterward that she understood me nonetheless.

My heart pounds when a gynecologist, who is seeing a deaf couple for infertility treatment, raises his voice while I am interpreting. "What do they want?" he yells. "Stop signing, stop!" he orders. "Can't we go off the record like they do in the courtroom?" he demands to know. I figure he is flustered by the graphic description of their efforts to conceive, and even more frustrated by his assumed loss of control over the consultation. I have to inform the doctor in front of the couple that I cannot stop signing as long as they are in the room. My role is to speak everything the couple signs and to sign to them everything the doctor says. That is in the professional code of ethics that interpreters adhere to. We are not to edit or delete information. We are to convey messages in keeping with the intent of the speaker. Skilled interpreters develop techniques to smooth over some of the disparities between the two cultures. Still, it cannot always be done.

Throughout my career I have been in scores of settings with deaf people—on joyous as well as distressing occasions. I've been there many times to push through contractions with deaf mothers giving birth, to sign through my tears, "It's a boy." I've been there to see deaf parents smile when a teacher reports how well their children are doing in school. I have seen the terror of a deaf glaucoma patient who gave one blind and swollen eye to surgical removal and then experienced the rewarding aftermath when a perfectly matched prosthesis was fit against the good eye. My heart soared while interpreting an award presentation to a deaf employee for exemplary attention to detail. I felt pride when a deaf juror deliberated through my hands and voice while performing his civic duty.

When the words flow back and forth through my hands, it is as though the notes to a song are inscribed in my heart. I take away those songs with me every day, the happy ones and the somber ones. That is my role in a world full of communication barriers.

• • • • •

Leaving the hospital, after witnessing Anthony's passing, I zipped my jacket up again. The noonday sun had taken the edge off the morning's chill. I felt light-headed and shaky from hunger. There was still time to drop off the nail gun and get the plans to the electrician and the plumber. I could eat in the car on my way back to the mountains. Bert would be waiting for me.

Bert's second Rocky Mountain winter.

Midas Touch

B ert returned home the second week of January. I was eager to resume our routine of lessons and wanted to include John and Mary, whom I hadn't worked with since Bert's accident. I was also anxious to talk to them about what had been on my mind during the period of working with Bert at the Life Care Center. I felt that Bert had the potential to become fluent in reading sign language, but for that to happen we'd need additional people who could sign to him. If more of his interactions were in sign language, it would hasten the probability of his fluency—and that would enhance his life immeasurably.

When I brought up the idea to Mary of bringing more signers into Bert's life, I was pleased to hear that she and John had been looking to hire someone to help Bert at home. Their focus, however, had been on finding someone who could learn to use the braille machine. They hadn't thought about hiring a person who knew sign.

"Well, why not maximize the benefit of your expenditure and hire someone who could sign?" I suggested. Although receptive, they didn't know of anyone, and most of the people I knew who could sign lived an hour or more away. It would be hard to find someone with sign skills who would drive that far to work with an elderly, late-deafened blind man for only a few hours a week.

We put our heads together to find someone. A few days later, the person's name came to me like a lightening bolt. I thought of Jean Kelly, an interpreter in our area who was friendly and easy going. I couldn't wait to tell John and Mary. Additionally, a workshop for interpreters and support-service providers for the deaf-blind was coming up at a local community college. I had attended workshops like this before and thought Bert might benefit from the experience. He would be exposed to many people using sign language there. I would tell them about this, too, after my lesson with Bert.

It had only been a couple of days since I had seen him at the Life Care Center, but I found Bert a new person when I arrived. The familiar halo was conspicuously absent, replaced by a soft neck brace. The only traces of the halo were the nearly healed scabs on each side of his forehead where the screws had been. Without the stiff posture forced by the halo, Bert seemed comfortable for the first time in a long while. The new Bert took the initiative when he said, "Diane, I've been thinking about our sign language lessons and there are some things I want to work on." He pulled a folded paper out of his shirt pocket and handed it to me. He had typed a list of words he wanted to review titled, "Word Sign I Forgot." He had twenty or so words listed in alphabetical order: *about, all, better, change, finish, introduce, no, yes . . .*

His new concerted attention on sign language took me by surprise. I had been accustomed to redirecting our conversations back to sign language when Bert would lead us off onto topics that captivated his interest. This time he was directly focused on sign language and *he* was initiating the lesson.

We worked our way down his list. I thought it interesting that he had included the signs for *yes* and *no*. For so many years, the family had used his tapping system for *yes* and *no*. During months of working with Bert it seemed these two signs just wouldn't imprint on his mind. But today he wanted them. So in spite of the fact that I had become a convert to the knee-tapping, we practiced the sign for *yes*—a simple up-and-down shake of the fist, like a head nodding—and *no*—a slurring of the letters *n* and *o*, which taps the index and second fingertips against the thumb. When we finished practicing all the words on Bert's list, we started on mine. I kept lists, too, of signs we needed to review and new ones I wanted to teach him.

With this sudden leap in progress, it seemed fitting that the deaf-blind workshop was coming up at this time. When I mentioned it to Mary, along with the possibility of hiring Jean Kelly, she was in favor. So were John and Bert. Two weeks later the four of us attended the workshop, along with Jean, who was newly hired to help with Bert.

The workshop instructor was Barb Coffan, the same woman Mary contacted when she was first looking for a sign language teacher. Barb's personality radiated enthusiasm, and she had a knack for making people feel valued and comfortable. Among her twenty-five workshop participants were several deaf people with varying degrees of vision loss, each of whom required a different mode of communication. Bert's primary mode was via the braille machine. He was still only a "beginner" to tactile sign language. A deaf woman with low vision used sign language but she needed to see it at a close range. Another woman, who had only a tunnel of vision, used a tracking method where she held onto the signer's wrist so she could follow where the signs moved. The other participants were sign language interpreters or support-service providers who worked with deaf-blind people. Barb accommodated everyone's communication needs by providing an interpreter for the deaf participants as well as an individual interpreter for each deaf-blind participant.

Bert sat at his own table with his braille machine, reading along as volunteers began taking turns typing out Barb's presentation to him. As was his habit, he read aloud as he interpreted the raised dots. "Read silently" were the last words we heard him say. He was participating in his first live group experience in almost twenty years.

During the workshop, we practiced on each other using several different methods of communication. One technique entailed drawing letters with a finger on the person's arm or hand. Another technique, called Tadoma, involved placing one hand on the side of the speaker's face and throat to feel the vibrations as she talked while we simultaneously traced the movement of her lips with our thumb. Helen Keller was known for her skill in this method of lipreading. It is rarely used today.

We learned appropriate techniques for guiding a deaf-blind person. Barb demonstrated with a volunteer while we watched. "You never push a blind person ahead of you," she said. "Rather, you allow him to take your arm and walk slightly behind you. This way he can follow your natural body movements while turning, stopping, or stair climbing." She told us it is important to warn the deaf-blind person when we're taking him onto an escalator. When we want him to enter a vehicle, we place his hand on the roof so he knows where it is. "Then he won't bang his head getting in," she said. "If another person comes up and starts talking to you, let the deaf-blind person know who it is and what he's saying. To be his link to the world, you need to let him know what's happening around him at all times."

Bert had never been around so many fluent signers. It was also the first time he was to meet another deaf-blind person. Barb asked him through the braille machine if he wanted to meet Francine. "She is also deaf-blind," Barb typed.

"I sure would," Bert said. He reached for his cane at his side and slowly pushed himself up away from the table. An interpreter led Bert over to Francine and directed his hand onto hers. "Is this Francine?" he asked. The interpreter tapped him twice. Another interpreter signed his question to Francine, who was using the tracking method. Francine's tunnel vision allowed her to see, though only through a peephole. When her interpreter's hand movements crossed her line of sight, Francine raised her hand to take the interpreter's wrist. Holding on this way, she followed the movements with her remaining sight.

"Francine," Bert said, "it's so good to meet you. Were you born deaf and blind?" His voice was nervous and shaky. Francine's interpreter signed his questions. "Where did you go to school?"

"Me, school, CSDB," she signed. Bert's interpreter signed Francine's answers into his hand, but Bert didn't understand the interpreter. Still, he had more questions. "Was school hard for you?" he asked.

Bert only understood the *yes* and *no* answers from the interpreter—nothing else. Nevertheless, I could sense the power in that moment for him. As a number of us wiped tears, I led Bert to the lectern where he began a speech about his life and struggles with the deterioration of his vision and hearing. He spoke nostalgically of the profession he had to give up. And he fondly remembered his wife and recognized his family for their support, which allowed him to push on, even more determined, to get to

Diane signs to Bert on a sunny winter day. As the wind blew snow from the roof, Bert remarked delightedly, "Oh, it's snowing!"

where he was. At the end, Barb orchestrated a group hug so Bert could feel the presence of all of us.

Bert inspired people at the workshop just as he had at the Life Care Center, the hospital, and everywhere he went. But this time he, too, came away enlivened. His thoughts afterward led him to a revelation. He called it the "Midas Touch." For Bert, the Midas Touch was something he had been missing in his life for almost forty years, until coming to live with John and Mary. It was the discovery of another one of his senses that made him feel complete. The Midas Touch had to do with feel, but it went deeper than that. It related to the depth of meaning communicated through human touch.

Marvin, an aide at the Life Care Center, was one of the persons whose actions helped Bert come to know the value of the Midas Touch. Marvin helped Bert shave when Bert first arrived. Late at night, when the halo interfered with Bert's sleep, Marvin would find Bert reading his braille magazines in the dark. He would sit down and talk to Bert using the braille machine. Bert got to know Marvin this way. Thereafter, whenever Bert was in physical therapy or in the dining room, Marvin would identify himself by reaching out to touch Bert's cheek in a gesture of shaving. This simple gesture gave Bert a picture of his environment by knowing who was in his midst, making Bert feel noticed and included in the mainstream of life. Bert could respond, "Hi there, Marvin. How are Cindy and the kids?"

The revelation of the Midas Touch was so important to Bert that he wrote an article about it and sent it to friends and to Barb Coffan. He said the Midas Touch offers a deaf-blind person perspective on his surroundings— something paramount to a person's joy in life. His Midas Touch consisted of three principles people needed to know before interacting with someone deaf-blind.

"First," he said, "identify yourself and make certain that we know who you are before you proceed to speak with us." Many times Bert had had the embarrassing experience of saying something to someone and finding out later that he had said it to the wrong person. "Second, provide us with enough information to enable us to have a mental picture of our immediate environment. Third, maintain physical contact with us to let us know that you are still there." For Bert, these three things made communication possible. To him it made life more fun.

Macaroon Cookies

Jean Kelly became a key player in Bert's immersion into sign language. Bert and Jean initially spent their time taking walks and playing honeymoon bridge. At first, their communication was halting and disjointed, as Bert's sign skills were still basic and Jean didn't know what signs I had taught him. She was groping in the dark (as was Bert) trying out words. Sometimes Bert understood her signs and sometimes he didn't. Consequently, he did most of the talking on their walks, while Jean kept trying out signs.

One day as they trudged down the dirt road toward the Riedels' house, Bert asked Jean a question. Unfortunately, it wasn't a question she could answer simply with one or two hand taps. *Yes* or *no* taps didn't work if you wanted to say, "I don't know." She tried to sign that she didn't know the answer, but Bert didn't understand her. Instinctively, she lifted his hands and set them on her shoulders, shrugging them in an exaggerated fashion. "Oh, you don't know," he said, and let out a hearty laugh. "That was like Charlie Chaplin!"

Jean's body language spoke volumes to Bert. It was the "Midas Touch" he had come to realize as so meaningful. Over time, in addition to their walks and card games, Jean added sign language instruction. She and I became his team of sign teachers. Now, including John and Mary,

Bert had four people signing to him. Bert loved it. He proclaimed to me one day, "I'm in Signland!"

About this time another Jean, a middle-aged woman from Conifer, came into Bert's life. Jean Dent had been thinking of volunteering with older people when she spotted Mary's advertisement in the local newspaper: *Family looking for a companion to spend time with an older deaf-blind man who likes to play bridge.* Jean Dent couldn't imagine how someone deaf-blind could play bridge nor could she imagine herself playing bridge with such a person. She passed over the ad. Months later, through the Mountain Resource Center, she heard about Bert again. "He likes to swim and hike and go out to eat," the volunteer coordinator told her. The more she thought about this man, the more curious she became about him. She liked to swim and hike, too, so she called John and Mary.

As it turned out, Jean Dent lived within walking distance of the Riedels, so she went over to meet them, nervous at first. Jean always felt nervous about meeting new people; however, she was immediately intrigued when she heard Bert playing the piano. Her first visit with them put her at ease, and Jean began spending time with Bert once a week. What transpired over the next few months surprised her. Jean had expected to be the one giving. But what she got back was so much more.

"The first time John and I took Bert swimming together, I sat on the bleachers and watched Bert swim, afraid to take my eyes off him for fear that something bad might happen," Jean recalled. After several weeks, she grew more comfortable taking Bert to the pool and even began swimming with him. Jean hadn't been swimming in a long time. With Bert, she found herself enjoying it again.

She rekindled her creative side as well. Upon hearing that Bert liked macaroon cookies, she whipped up her first batch and took them over to Bert. He was so delighted with the cookies that Jean started baking her great-grand-mother's orange bread and cooking other recipes she hadn't made in years.

During this revival of Jean's homemaking skills, Mary asked her if she knew how to sew. Mary had been looking for a pack that would allow Bert's hands to be free. "It's not safe for him to be carrying things when he walks up and down the stairs," she said. Jean had never sewn a pack before. Without a pattern, she and Mary came up with a design uniquely suited for Bert. Jean dusted off her sewing machine and surprised Bert with her creation only a few days later. It was a yellow canvas knapsack, simply styled with a Velcro closure at the top. He could fit his braille *New York Times* inside, along with a few toiletries, and slip easily into its two shoulder straps. A button sewn in the corner let Bert know which side of the sack faced outward. His gracious praise of her thoughtfulness and skill inspired Jean to keep the sewing machine out and start sewing again.

• • • • •

As spring approached, Bert's life was blossoming with activities and friends. One friend was noticeably absent, however—Peggy Grant, the volunteer at the Life Care Center with whom Bert had enjoyed many long talks. Bert missed Peggy tremendously. Apparently, Peggy felt the gap, too, because she called Mary to ask if she could visit. Mary welcomed Peggy to their home, and in a stitch of time Peggy and Bert picked up their talks right where they had left off. From then on, each time Peggy came over, Mary had Peggy's favorite tea with a pretty teapot and mug sitting on the table next to the brailler. There was also honey, bought especially for Peggy.

Peggy and Bert often engaged in leisurely strolls along the road in front of the house. Because Peggy didn't know sign language and was unable to talk to Bert on the walks, she thought to enhance the experience with sensory stimulation. One time she led him over to a tree to feel the trunk and the pine cones. She picked a dandelion for him to identify with a sniff. He held the dandelion close to his nose and inhaled deeply. It left a giant yellow smudge on the end of his nose. When she described it to him later at the braille machine, Bert had a good laugh about it.

Bert taught Peggy how to play honeymoon bridge using his braille cards, just as he had taught Jean Kelly, Vera Feistal, and Jean Dent. At each game, Peggy watched Bert deal the cards and identify his hand by feeling the braille dots. He always organized his cards into four piles according to suit. He carefully counted the number in each pile and memorized them. Then he was ready to play. Bert never missed an opportunity to encourage his novice opponent by telling her how quickly she was picking up the game. He complimented Peggy on her "natural strategy."

Bert thrived on a challenging game of bridge. He always made his opponents feel smart, so they played smart. He told his opponents that they had an incredible memory for each card that was played. The truth was, Bert kept track out loud of the cards played, so he was continually reminding the other players. His favorite play was his "Dirty Bertie." If he had only one trump card, he led with it, forcing his opponents to play two of their precious trump cards. Most of his bridge companions quickly and goodheartedly learned to play his Dirty Bertie trick back on him.

Bert and his youngest friend, Vera, also spent time together before she went off to college. Sometimes Vera drove him to the pool. One day while sitting on the bleachers watching Bert swim, her thoughts drifted off to three of her friends, each of whom had attempted suicide. Vera told me she'd also been thinking about members of her own family whose lives were in turmoil as well, when she saw Bert accidentally bang his head against the concrete wall of the pool. Unshaken, Bert kept on swimming. His determination to continue, no matter what, made

Peggy Grant and Jean Kelly pose with Bert and I.

Vera realize that life is all about overcoming obstacles and never giving up. "It's just a matter of making choices," she remarked.

When Bert and Vera returned home from swimming, the topic of discussion turned to Bert's work in dentistry. He began to explain the proper method of brushing and flossing when their time together ran out and Vera had to leave. The next time Vera came over, Bert resumed the conversation exactly where it ended the time before. Taking a piece of floss from his pocket, he assured Vera he had just washed his hands as he had her open her mouth and proceeded to demonstrate "the best way to floss."

Another time Bert related an incident at a party when he was introduced to a woman who, unbeknownst to Bert, was wearing a wig. As the two of them were saying hello, Bert reached up, as he always did, and patted the woman's head. It shocked them all when her wig came off. "I'll never forget that one!" Bert said smiling, amused by his own story. Soon he and Vera were bent over in hysterics. After they'd recovered, Bert said, "Let's have some more fun with a couple hands of bridge." He didn't let her get away before teasing her with his Dirty Bertie trick. He followed his victory with a mischievous smile. "Will you ever forgive me?"

Typing into the brailler, Vera answered playfully, "Never."

Words of Wisdom

One year into our lessons, I took my two teenagers over to meet Bert. It was March 1999, and the kids were on spring vacation. The sound of Dvorak's *New World Symphony* greeted us as we opened the door. The kids followed me into the dining room where we found Bert at the piano. The master with snowy-white hair swayed ever so slightly to the music he was playing. Heather, Matthew, and I stood near him, relishing the impression until the last note. I tapped Bert's arm to let him know we were there.

"Who is this? Diane?" he asked.

"Yes," I said, tapping him twice.

His face lit up. "Oh, how *are* you? Let me get my stick." He leaned down to feel for the cane at his feet. "It's good to see you." He scooted to the end of the piano bench and with a grunt pushed himself to a stand.

"I d-i-d bring my children. T-h-e-y want meet you," I signed into his hand. "This is M-a-t-t-h-e-w." I directed his hand to Matt's.

"Nice to meet you, Matthew," he said in an interested tone. He shook hands with his right while reaching with his left to touch the top of Matt's head. Bert liked to "see" how tall people were. "And where is Heather?"

Heather extended her hand to him. Bert greeted her in the same manner.

"Heather and Matthew, help yourselves to a drink from the refrigerator and come sit at the table," he told them. Heather took a can of Coke from the refrigerator, but Matthew didn't drink pop. He pulled a chair out from the table and sat down. I led Bert to the table where we settled ourselves around his braille machine. I started signing to Bert, interpreting the kids' answers to his myriad questions. After a few minutes, Matthew initiated communication directly with Bert using the brailler.

"I'm writing an English composition. I wonder if you could tell me something about you that I could share with my class."

Bert thought for a moment. "Let me share a little of my life's history," he said. Matthew glanced over at me and sunk down in his chair as if preparing to sit through a boring lecture. In a matter of minutes, however, the kids were mesmerized. Bert held them spellbound for the next hour.

"I was born in 1911, in Chicago," he began. "My father, Adolf, came to the U.S. from Holland. He was a doctor working in general practice on the west side of Chicago. My mother, Marie, stayed home and raised my two brothers, Wesley and Hank, and me. We went to a private Lutheran school not too far from our apartment. Our classes were small and the students' parents were mostly doctors and ministers. The administrators were strict Germans and they didn't allow any fooling around or disobedience, so we learned our German and learned not to defy the elders.

"Although I could hear and see as a youngster, as early as six years old I remember twisting knots in my hair as I strained to understand the teacher." He explained that the children were seated alphabetically in the first grade, so with the name Riedel, he found himself in the back row.

Without realizing what he was doing, he moved closer and closer to the teacher to watch her face and lips. It was the only way he could understand her.

"The kids at school laughed at me because I tripped over things and appeared clumsy. The teachers accused me of not paying attention. Their reactions confused me because I didn't know anything was wrong—I didn't realize I had hearing and vision problems.

Heather and Matthew sat quiet and still with their eyes on Bert. The old storyteller edged forward a bit in his chair, staring straight ahead. Bert loved an audience. He hardly moved as he spoke except for his hand, which checked from time to time for new dots on the brailler. Reserved and polite, my kids were quiet. They didn't speak much to someone they'd just met. Heather was too shy to ask Bert a question yet.

"In the neighborhood, the kids formed gangs," Bert went on. "There were many poor immigrants from Europe, and most of the kids were rough. They would beat up kids from other gangs and steal their money. You had to be brave or you'd get hurt. Once, a big bully taunted me with a metal rod. I faced him and put up my fist. I said, 'Do you want to fight?' The tormentor ran away, but that taught me an important lesson—to never run away from anything life threw at me."

The kids looked at each other, smiling at Bert's fearlessness. Bert told us he was especially close to his brother Wes. They walked to school together down the "big road" that passed by a movie theater. They read the marquis and other signs as they walked by, but Bert couldn't see them nearly as well as Wes. "Wes corrected me when I read them wrong," he said. "I just accepted it. At the dinner table my brothers would say, 'Bert's slow.' Other times they said,

'Bert hears when he wants to hear.'" They seemed annoyed that Bert didn't hear all the time—that he seemed to tune out when it was convenient for him. They didn't realize that Bert could only catch what people were saying when he could see their faces.

"Wes and I spent most of our time together outdoors. Sometimes we walked to the golf course to play golf. When I couldn't see where I had hit the ball, Wes patiently helped me find it."

Matthew interrupted Bert. Leaning forward in his chair, he typed a question into the brailler. I directed Bert's hand to the machine so he could read it. "Did you play other sports besides golf?"

"I didn't really play much golf," he replied. "Mostly I played basketball. In spite of my problems, I got involved with the basketball team. I loved the game and wanted to be good but it was frustrating. When the other players passed the ball to me, I'd often miss it or drop it. I thought everyone had the same difficulties. I was competitive and overcompensated by going too fast and trying too hard. I was pretty good actually, though I was never an ace player."

Bert told us that it was in music where he excelled. "I developed a love of music from my father. He loved music and he was the one who encouraged me when I began learning the piano in junior high school. He'd take us boys to the Chicago Symphony Orchestra to hear classical music. I loved it and I wanted to imitate it. I played my first recital at age fourteen. The teacher heard me play Beethoven's 'Minuet in G,' and then he hooked me up with a classmate who played the violin. We practiced a duet together and then played it for the school. That sparked my serious interest in music."

We also learned that Bert excelled academically—earning the honor of delivering the commencement speech at his high school graduation. But at the University of Chicago, Bert met his Waterloo.

"I couldn't understand what the teachers were saying," he said. "There were too many students in the classes and the teachers were too far away for me to read their lips. I had tunnel vision by then and I was bumping into people. They'd complain and say, 'Look where you're going.' Often I misinterpreted what people said, and many thought I was just a snob. I was in serious difficulty. Still, I made it through college and dental school. I practiced dentistry until I could no longer see. I had to hang up my dental tools at age forty-three."

I looked to see if the kids had any questions, but Heather only sipped her Coke. Matthew slunk down in his chair again as Bert unfolded more of his past. I held Bert's hand to let him know we were still there listening. He shared what happened after he gave up dentistry.

"I enrolled in a training program for the blind on the south side of Chicago. I traveled there by train, memorizing each stop, in case I wouldn't hear the conductor when he called out State Street, where I got off." From there, Bert took a streetcar the rest of the way to the school. He used his remaining bit of sight and a white cane to walk the last few blocks with a satchel full of braille books hanging from his shoulder. He swung the cane from side to side to uncover obstacles in his way, mindful to be careful as he walked through the run-down neighborhood.

"The school was located in a house that had been converted to a residential program for blind adults," Bert explained. "It included vocational training where we were taught to make things with our hands." Bert lived at the school Monday through Friday, immersing himself in what he needed to learn to prepare for his future. He acquired woodworking skills and made dining room tables and cane-back chairs. Through his tunnel of vision, Bert could manage the saw and see the furniture pieces. And he could make out the face of the director, Mr. Dickinson, who was blind himself.

Bert told us he learned to read braille at the school in preparation for the time when all would become dark. "When I first started learning braille, it was so hard. I got discouraged and felt the pain in my fingers. Almost in tears, I'd say, 'What letter is this?' But I kept at it—I learned it, though I could only read the dots with one finger." Decades later Bert still used only his index finger to read braille. Those who learn braille at an early age read it with two hands and several fingers. Their other fingers act as guides to keep them in a straight line.

Bert also learned to use a braillewriter, the Perkins Brailler. "Braille writing uses contractions," he said, demonstrating in the air how some keys are pushed at the same time, in different combinations of the six dots that compose all braille characters. "Variations of one to six dots in a cell form letters, and one or two letters together can be symbols for words. For example: *fr* means 'friend'; *y l my fr* means 'you like my friend.' I found it complicated and the machine was too bulky to carry around. I later discarded it. Now I read a grade two braille, which uses abbreviations like *i*, which means 'in.' It's faster than grade one braille, which spells out every letter, though it's still slower than you can read with your eyes."

Bert's mention of the braillewriter reminded me of my junior high school—of how we made way for the blind students who hauled their bulky machines down the hallways. As I pictured Bert carrying his machine, he recounted some pleasant memories of attending the vocational school.

"I was walking to school one day, when a man asked me where I was going. I told him, 'To the Chicago School for the Blind.'[15] He said he knew where it was and then he kindly called a cab for me. Another time a little black girl met me on the street corner. She took my hand and led me across the street to the school. I could have done it myself, but it made her happy to do that for me. Then she said good-bye and ran away."

Bert then alluded to something unpleasant that happened—something that still bothered him. "A friend at the school let me know that someone was spreading rumors about me for something I apparently had said in the washroom. I never found out what it was I had said wrong. I often got confused like that because I couldn't hear well." Bert dismissed the unpleasant memory. "Some people just have mean streaks in them and they take advantage of weaker ones," he said.

By now, I thought my kids might be getting restless and ready to leave. But when I looked over at them, they were fully engaged with Bert. Heather asked, "Mom, did he ever have a guide dog?"

I took Bert's hands. "H-e-a-t-h-e-r want know i-f you d-i-d have g-u-i-d-e dog."

"Yes," he replied. "In 1968, I took my first airplane ride and went to Rochester, Michigan, to a training institute funded by the Lions Clubs called 'Leader Dogs for the Blind.' I stayed there for several weeks to be trained and matched to a dog."

Bert related how his dog, Duchess, became his companion as well as his aide for independent mobility. "The administrators at the training institute were reluctant at first to accept me into the program because of my dual disability," he told us. "Blind masters must have very good orientation skills. I had to be responsible for knowing where I was and where I was going. Dogs can't make decisions about where to go and they don't understand traffic lights. The blind master needs to depend on his own hearing for cues and then use voice or hand commands to tell the dog where to go. But the dogs are trained to refuse a directive if there's a hazard."

Duchess was a German Shepherd with a black stripe down her back. Although Bert's hearing wasn't good, he and his shepherd painstakingly practiced on the training course in the orchard of the institute and on the streets of Rochester, until they proved to be a competent team. In the end, Bert was permitted to take Duchess home. "She went everywhere with me—to the bank and to the post office. We walked eight miles every day. I had her for ten years."

As Bert's story seemed to be winding down, the kids and I were gripped by the struggles Bert experienced as his hearing deteriorated.

"I had difficulty following what people were saying, and social situations were becoming uncomfortable for me as well as for others," Bert said. It was just easier for everyone to let Bert do the talking. He recalled one sad occasion with some friends in Chicago. "The husband and wife were old friends of ours. He was a nice guy who made a good living as an accountant. They had a nice house and gave nice parties, but after I lost all of my sight and most of my hearing, our relationship with them changed. They invited us over one evening. When my friend met me at the door, he turned me around and walked me backward into the house. He sat me down into a comfy chair and left me there for an hour. That was all he knew to do. He didn't even try to talk to me. I knew he felt sorry for me. That was the way it became with everyone.

"I didn't know how to educate people about what I needed because *I* didn't know. I pretended I could hear, though I couldn't understand enough to join in on conversations. So I didn't have too many friends. People thought I had given up and didn't care. I just couldn't explain my situation. Then I had to give up my dog, too, because I could no longer hear the traffic on the streets to give her instructions. We had to put her out to pasture. I didn't like that part of my life . . . it was too sad. I'd been solving problems all my life, but I couldn't solve my social problems."

Bert concluded on a more cheerful note. "In 1940, I made a pledge to myself to always remain positive," he said. "For the last two years, I've been working to find ways to enjoy life. Although I broke my neck, it wasn't a bad experience because I got to meet some wonderful people. I've found sign language and now I can connect with people again."

I don't know what my kids were feeling, but I had tingles all over. We each began to stir in our seats as Bert said, "Well, Matthew, that's how I got here. My life's been a fruitful journey because of the people I've met along the way. Now tell me, what do you plan to pursue in school?"

"I don't really know yet," he typed.

"No matter what you do, you must find something you truly love, and do it well. As you grow older you'll start to understand what's important in life and what happiness really is. It is a blessing to sit outside on a beautiful sunny day in good health and appreciate your surroundings. Find whatever it is that makes you happy and hold onto it with your dear life. Always put your best effort into everything you do, and you'll never need to look back with regret."

As we said good-bye to Bert, I saw tears in Matt's eyes. Bert had left an impression on my seventeen-year-old that would probably last a lifetime. I learned the depth of it when I read the English composition Matthew subsequently wrote. It began like this:

> *Wise men have been considered sacred in all of ancient history. The elite group of elders has run over fiery coals in glimpses of hell and gracefully danced through shades of heaven through their experiences. In our current society, that earned respect has been slightly forgotten. The lust for the dollar bill has diminished the true purpose in life, and is something which I had to be reminded of through the life experiences of a brilliant 87-year-old man. In an unbelievably subtle way, his story taught me more about what to look for in my next phase of life than any class or textbook. It was as if I was looking right through his eyes into God's. Like I had found a passageway to a place that tells the secrets to life. I left there feeling like I had been sent a gift.*

Tunnel Vision

At different times Bert shared more with me about his past, living with increasing tunnel vision. He talked about his childhood when his family finally realized he wasn't merely "slow." And he reminisced about his marriage to Helen, whom he loved deeply, and how they struggled together with his Usher Syndrome.

In grade school, Bert's father had taken him for an eye examination. But neither he nor Bert's mother ever told him whether the doctor discovered anything. "I suspect now that my parents knew about my problem and that my mother did worry, but she was busy taking care of the house and raising two other sons," Bert said. "My dad was a laid-back optimist who never seemed to worry about anything. He made investments without even investigating them. If a person offered him a cigar, he'd buy whatever he was selling. My parents *must* have been concerned about my problems. They simply didn't know what to do about them."

Consequently, Bert went through the rest of childhood and high school unknowingly compensating for his deficiencies. When it was time to go to college, the Depression hit and Adolph, his father, lost all of his savings. Bert had to take out a loan to attend the University of Chicago.

"I didn't do well in the competitive environment of the university," he said. "I understood by then that my hearing was diminishing, and it was presenting an even bigger challenge than my poor eyesight. But after I graduated with my science degree and transferred to the University of Illinois Dental School, classes were smaller and more manageable. I kept up with the academics by copying my classmates' notes. It made up for the lectures I couldn't hear."

Bert confronted different challenges in dental school. "I was required to make a wax carving of a tooth. The dental lab had dim light and I needed strong light to see what I was doing. One day I took the carving from the lab downstairs to a place where the light was better. The teacher didn't understand why I did this and he reprimanded me for leaving the lab. My poor vision was an annoying problem at that time, but I think it was my inadequate hearing that held me back even more. If I'd been able to hear better in college, I might have graduated Phi Beta Kappa," Bert said regretfully.

Though Bert had been disappointed in not graduating with academic distinction from college, his father had been proud and rewarded his son with a grand piano. With the new piano, Bert immersed himself in earnest study of Beethoven's sonatas, simultaneous with his medical studies—the end of which culminated with a dental internship. The internship was in Rochester, New York, at a children's dental clinic where the Eastman Kodak company was helping underprivileged children get access to dental care. Bert worked there for $25 a week, examining young patients and developing X-rays.

He saved enough money from his internship so that later, in 1937, when a friend helped him find an office, he was able to start his own dental practice. "I opened my office in Lombard, a suburb twenty-five miles west of Chicago, when the town only had about ten thousand people. There was no industry there to speak of and I sat and waited for customers for nearly three months. I'd do a cleaning for $3 one day and pull a tooth for $3 on another day. Nobody had any money at that time. Thankfully, the Depression ended and people finally started coming."

In the autumn of the following year, Bert started walking to the nearby library that was housed in an old Victorian home adjacent to Lilacia Park. The simple two-story house had originally been owned by Colonel William Plum, a Civil War veteran who loved books and gardens. The colonel started cultivating the garden next to his house with two species of lilac bushes he'd brought back from Europe. When he died in 1927, he bequeathed his home to the town, and it became the Helen Plum Memorial Library, named after his wife. The colonel's well-manicured gardens became Lilacia Park, where today three hundred varieties of lilacs grow, and people come from all over to see them in the spring.

The library offered "memberships," so one day with the intent of opening one, Bert climbed the stairs of its pillared front porch and sauntered into the main area. There his eyes met those of a tall blond girl at the desk who looked up and smiled at him. "She was an apparition of loveliness," Bert recollected. She was Helen May Johnson. Bert pretended to peruse the books while he watched her work. In Helen, Bert saw the image he had longed for in a mate.

In time, they struck up a friendship and Bert visited the library more often. The two began taking walks together along the stone paths in Lilacia Park and sat on the benches in the shade of a tree, talking about books. They spent hours enjoying each other's company, yet Bert never mentioned his hearing problem. He was twenty-six years old, and although he was at times unsure of his hearing, he was quite sure this was the woman he wanted to marry. Eleven months after they met, Bert and Helen were married—in 1939, by Bert's brother Wes, who had become a Methodist minister.

Bert and Helen moved into an old Colonial home on Maple Street near the library where Helen worked. Later they bought a car—a red Pontiac, because Helen liked it and she was the one who did the driving. In time, as the Lombard community came to know Dr. Riedel as a respected dentist, Bert and Helen started a family. First born was their daughter Sue. Then came Marcia and John.

On the outside, everything seemed wonderful. At thirty-five, Bert was in the prime of his life. He had a beautiful family and a successful dental career. But inside, he was silently worried. As his peripheral sight was receding and his hearing diminishing, he gave into a growing suspicion that something devastating was happening to him.

An ophthalmologist in Elmhurst, Illinois, diagnosed the problem as retinitis pigmentosa, a condition in which the light-sensitive cells of the eye, the rods, and the cones gradually lose their ability to pick up images. The doctor gave no cause for the deteriorating retinas. He merely said that they would eventually leave Bert totally blind.

The diagnosis addressed only Bert's eye problem. There was no recognition of the hearing loss or the underlying condition that had plagued him all of his life. It would be many more years, until after Marcia's marriage to an ophthalmologist, that a label was attached to his dual impairment: Usher Syndrome—the result of inheriting a recessive Usher gene from each of his parents. Like the estimated one in seventy-five who carry one normal and one Usher gene, Bert's parents had been unaware they were carriers. In the most common type of Usher Syndrome, children are born deaf and learn sign language before they lose their vision to retinitis pigmentosa.

Retinitis pigmentosa begins with impaired night vision and balance problems. As the condition progresses, it slowly erodes peripheral vision, leaving only a tunnel of vision. Although the central vision may remain sharp for a long time, the retina eventually becomes less able to use light and send information to the brain. Total blindness is the result. There is no cure.

In Bert's case, having the more uncommon type of Usher Syndrome, the gaps in his vision and hearing were mild during childhood. He was able to learn speech and acquire most of his education before his hearing deteriorated in his early twenties. He compensated for the hearing loss by lipreading. At that point, people still thought Bert had more hearing than he did—they didn't realize he was getting by because of lipreading. They noticed his vision loss more.

After learning he would become totally blind, Bert predicted he had less than ten years left to practice dentistry. Knowing his time was running out, he finally disclosed his worries to Helen about his affliction. After nine years of marriage, he told her they would need to make a dramatic shift in their plans for their future. He thought they should move to Maine.

Bert's brother Wes had a ministry in Augusta, Maine, and he encouraged Bert and Helen to come east to be near him and his wife. After investigating work possibilities, Bert discovered that many people in Maine couldn't afford dental care and had teeth in poor condition. They needed dentures. As long as his tunnel vision remained sharp, Bert believed he could make the change from doing the fine work of small fillings to fitting the larger-size prostheses, which were more easily manipulated. He would still be able to work and support his family. Ultimately, the Riedels left their home and friends in Lombard, in hopes of a better future in New England.

A Desperate Plea

Although Bert never said so, I gathered that the years in Maine were bittersweet. Settled in Westbrook, sixty miles from his brother in Augusta, Bert knew he was losing his sight and his hearing. Yet he was determined to make the best out of each day. While he could still see, he took his family on adventurous outings across New England, sometimes accompanied by Wes's family. The two families developed a deep relationship during this period.

I learned about their joyful times from Bert's niece, Marie, who wrote her recollections in a letter to me. She said it was always special when the two families united in Augusta for holidays. She and her sister were close in age to their cousins, Sue and Marcia. The four girls played with five-year-old John and doted on two-year-old Philip, the youngest addition to Bert's family. Marie wrote, "When the noise level got too high, I remember Bert saying to Wes, 'This is one advantage of being deaf. I just turn down my hearing aid and the kids don't bother me a bit.'" Marie remembered how Bert would tease his kids when he admonished them at dinner. "'Eat every carrot and pea on your plate,'" he'd say. The kids would giggle and respond, "'We can't pee on our plates, Daddy.'"

She recalled how Bert loved feigning that he didn't remember an off-color story and would tell everyone he was sure Helen knew it. Reluctantly, she'd tell it with a perfectly delivered punch line followed by a whopping measure of embarrassment. After everyone had stopped laughing, Bert would say, "Oh Helen, you can't tell that one! That's too racy!" It was Bert's playful amusement everyone enjoyed over and over.

Summer vacations together were their happiest times in Maine. Wes and Bert rented cottages nestled in the pines at Lake Sebago or Panther Pond. The kids swam and played on the sandy beaches while the adults relaxed in the beauty of the woods and water. As Marie described her memories of the adults' uproarious bridge games, the families' elaborately costumed skits, and everyone singing with Uncle Bert at the piano, I realized that Bert had a long history as a performer. I also saw that his love of the water went way back. "During the day Bert gave swimming lessons to the kids," Marie wrote. "He was a hard, but fair, taskmaster. He made sure we learned the crawl and the breaststroke and practiced breathing using his techniques."

Sometimes when things got too wild at the cottages, Bert and Wes would swim out toward the middle of the lake. They knew the children couldn't swim well enough to keep up with them, so they would stay out there a while, talking and laughing, far away from responsibilities. After their swim, they sat by the lake, indulging in a cigar. At night while the kids were in bed, Wes and Bert took another dip in the lake, with their wives, all giggling like kids themselves.

•　•　•　•　•

Into the 1950s, the times were not all joyful. Bert and Helen found themselves coping with the complications of Bert's blindness and hearing loss. Their future was uncertain because they didn't know how long Bert could continue his dental practice. He was depending on two hearing aids to hear his patients and working through a narrowing tunnel of vision. He relied on his dental assistant more and more.

"Helen had begun driving me to work," Bert told me, "because I was no longer confident about walking by myself. Twice at the crosswalk I had cars come so close that I felt the tires roll over my toes. I had bumps and bruises up and down my shins from banging into tables. I had gashes in my forehead from banging into door frames. I finally dropped to my knees in a desperate plea to my wife one day. I asked her to go back to school to get her teaching degree in the event that *she* would have to take over the breadwinning responsibilities."

"You're doing fine, Bert," was her answer to his plea. She still didn't grasp the gravity of the situation. Bert hadn't told her about the frightening times when he'd gotten lost walking around the neighborhood, sometimes finding himself in strange backyards. Or about the time he was swimming at Old Orchard Beach and thought he would drown because he'd lost sight of the shore. Luckily, he spotted some rocks sticking up six to ten feet out of the water. From the rocks he was able to construe the correct direction and swim back to where his feet met the sand.

All the while, Bert didn't talk about his fears with anyone. Instead, he kept adapting to his increasing disability and eventually moved his practice into his home, adding a storefront to the house on Main Street. Helen ultimately enrolled in school at Gorham State Teacher's College in Augusta.

During the years in Westbrook, when he wasn't fitting dentures, Bert spent many hours at his piano. As his eyesight continued to fade, he sat at the keys in rapt concentration, working to memorize his beloved pieces before the notes on the page dissolved in front of him. At dinner, when he began eating with a lamp to give more light to the shadows of food on his plate, it was evident that the time had come. Bert was no longer able to continue his dental practice. Resigned, he moved his family back to Lombard, grateful for the good times and support of Wes and his family.

• • • • •

Bert and Helen found Lombard the same quiet suburb that they had left nearly seven years before. They bought a home on Charlotte Street and Bert started vocational training at the residential program for the blind in Chicago. Helen got a job teaching sixth grade in Lombard. On the weekends, Bert took the train home to be with his family. After a year, he finished vocational training. Despite his new skills, Bert was determined to stay in the field of dentistry, a profession he still loved.

Working out of the house on Charlotte Street, Bert began writing articles from his sunroom desk. He wrote for a dental magazine, *Ask Oral Hygiene*, and with an assistant named Eloise, he started a mail-order business, selling X-ray films and other supplies to dentists. Eloise helped ship the supplies and did the bookkeeping. She ordered Bert's talking books and brailled materials. She read information to Bert and talked to him about current events. As he slipped further into the grips of Usher Syndrome, Eloise was the one who kept Bert connected to the world.

Helen and Bert eventually finished raising their four children in Lombard and proudly sent them all to college. With the kids grown and gone and Helen teaching school during the day, Bert had his afternoons alone. His vision had deteriorated more, to where he mostly saw only light and forms. The faces of his loved ones had faded away and smiles were lost. Memories of his visual world were frozen in time. He knew his hearing would be gone someday, too. Still, he had a little hearing left to enjoy his beloved music. He never wanted to give up the music.

"I went to the Zenith dealer and bought the highest quality phonograph money could buy at that time," he said. "I put the Zenith in the most important place in the house—in the living room across from my Chickering piano." The phonograph with its two front speakers fit inside a six-foot mahogany cabinet, with enough space inside for his stack of records.

"The kids had shown me how to work the buttons to raise or lower the volume. I would lay my head on a pillow right next to the speaker so the music poured through me while I imagined myself as the conductor." But just listening to the Zenith wasn't enough for Bert. He bought the musical scores and with a light and a magnifying glass held near the pages, he could make out the stanzas. Racing against time, he played the sonatas and played them again and again with his eyes closed until he played them from memory. When Helen came home from work and graded her students' papers at night, Bert lay on the floor next to the Zenith and listened more. "I wanted the music to last forever in my head."

Columbine

The phone rang at 11:35 a.m. on April 20, 1999. I'd already been on the phone most of the morning, coordinating last-minute travel arrangements for my son's soccer team. The boys were leaving in two days for a coaches' showcase tournament in Cincinnati. Andrew, Matthew's soccer coach, was on the line.

"Have you heard what's happening at Columbine?" Andrew asked. He was referring to the high school in our county and the atrocity that would soon be etched in our minds forever. "Turn on your TV," Andrew urged. "There's shooting, and pipe bombs are going off. I need to get in touch with Jeff, quick. Do you have his work number?"

Jeff was a parent of one of our players who attended Columbine. We had two players from that school—Derek, Jeff's son, and Zach. I hurried to look for the phone number and gave it to him as I walked over to the TV.

I got nothing else accomplished that day. What I saw kept me glued to the set. The scene of horror was being played out live. Terror-stricken students were running in lines out of the school with their hands behind their heads. I was hoping to catch a glimpse of Derek or Zach and Derek's younger sister, Lauren. Andrew and I phoned back and forth throughout the afternoon with updates on the whereabouts of the kids. Between calls with him and watching the ongoing newscast, I talked to parents and contacted players to let them know our soccer practice was being canceled.

At 3:30 p.m., Andrew called back. "Derek's okay. He was at the mall eating lunch. Zach made it safely out of the building, running from his math class, but we still haven't found Lauren."

I'd just hung up the phone when the director of the tournament in Cincinnati called. He recognized the name of Columbine and knew our team was from the area. The news of the high school shooters' carnage had already spread across the country. "We're aware of what's going on there," he said. "If there's anything we can do for your team, let us know."

"Thank you," I said. "It's terrible. We're all in shock, but our players are safe; our team is intact. We're just looking for one boy's sister."

By twilight, Lauren was finally accounted for. Later, her mother, Kate, my good friend, told me that Lauren had been in the cafeteria where the shooters began their violent rampage. Trying to get to the library where she thought she'd be safe, Lauren was pushed in another direction by a crowd of students escaping from the lunchroom. In the stampede she was shoved to the ground at the top of the stairs, stomped on, trampled, and knocked out. When she came to, bullets were flying and bouncing off of lockers in the hallway around her. She managed to get back on her feet, hearing the shooters yelling behind her. "It was hard to run," she cried, when her parents found her. "My chest was hurting." She sobbed as her weeping mother held her close.

Lauren never made it to the library where, in the end, most of the fatalities occurred. She was one of thirteen panicked students who burst out of the east door at the end of a long hallway. They all ran and jumped into a passing motorist's car. The driver took them to her home. By the time Lauren got her turn to use the woman's phone, she was in shock and hysterical. She didn't even know the address of the stranger's house to give to her dad. Kate had been frantically climbing over fences in the neighborhood around the school, searching for her daughter among the fifty or sixty kids at each house. Jeff was going house to house in another neighborhood trying to find Lauren after she called. Like Kate's family, the entire community was in chaos.

Two days later, our team was still shaken when we gathered at the airport. We soccer moms said good-bye and I love you to our pride-and-joys at the gate, thankful that our kids were alive and grief-stricken that fifteen families had just lost one of theirs. While we were concerned about the boys' emotional state, we left our precious cargo in the hands of the coaches and a couple of dads. The boys, glad to get away from the nightmare, put their focus—as they had been trained to do for years—on the soccer tournament. At midnight, Matthew called to say that they were still at the airport in Chicago, stranded by heavy rain. They were scheduled for an eight o'clock game the following morning. "They'll never make it," I told Jim.

The next day, as I was driving to the Riedels' house, I got a call from Zach's mom. She had just spoken with her son. "Did you hear about the game?" she asked me.

"No, I figured they missed it."

"They won!" she said. "They got to Cincinnati at three this morning and they made it to the eight o'clock game. They beat last year's national champion!"

Our kids were resilient and amazing. They still had two more games to play in the tournament. Suddenly, I was hopeful for them.

The TV was on at the Riedels' house when I arrived. I'd never seen it on before. The media was still covering Columbine extensively, four days after the tragedy, and I wondered whether Bert had any idea of the catastrophe that had befallen our community. He wasn't sitting at the kitchen table where he always waited for me. Mary was coming down from upstairs. She seemed as shuddered as I was. All abuzz, we spoke in bleary chatter over the noise of the television about what had happened. Sign language lessons were far from our minds.

"Bert was with me in the Jeep when I heard it on the radio," Mary said. "I was trying to listen to it but he was talking. I had to pull over so I could tell him that something terrible was happening. She had spelled, I h-e-a-r, r-a-d-i-o-, s-c-h-o-o-l, s-h-o-o-t-i-n-g. Bert had to wait to find out more about the terrible shootings until they got home to use the power brailler.

Bert and I talked a little about the tragedy when he came upstairs for our lesson. He was deeply saddened. He couldn't understand the senselessness and the terrible loss of such innocent lives. "I wish I could do something," he said.

"You *are* doing something," I signed, patting the silver and blue ribbon of the Columbine school colors he had pinned to his fleece jacket.

On May 1, a chilling photo on the front page of the Denver *Rocky Mountain News* said it all, so I shared it with Bert at our next lesson. "C-a-r-p-e-n-t-e-r from C-h-i-c-a-g-o did build some big crosses from w-o-o-d and did bring crosses here to Colorado." I fingerspelled the words he had not yet learned signs for. "He put all crosses on hill near school in C-l-e-m-e-n-t P-a-r-k." I described the photo in ASL: "Sun (going down), sky, orange, can see, far away hill."

I gestured the slope of the hill with my hand curving up from the left and down to the right. I made a cross with my two index fingers. As Bert felt my hands slowly make fifteen more crosses, setting each one an inch apart over my imaginary hill, we both choked up.

Stewed Tomatoes and Asparagus on Toast

Late in the spring John and Mary hired Andrea Duykers, a woman in her early fifties, to be a companion for Bert. As Jean Kelly, I, and volunteers Vera, Peggy, and Jean Dent continued to fill segments of his mornings and afternoons, there were times when John and Mary were not available to assist Bert with his correspondence and various needs. The couple no longer employed the housekeeper and cook who were hired upon Bert's arrival, so they were now spread thin. When someone referred them to Andrea, they warmed to her immediately. The twinkle of her dark brown eyes and her easy smile had that effect on people.

Andrea knew the fingerspelled alphabet and a few signs from a sign language class she took ten years earlier. Although she had no experience with deaf-blind persons, she had known some blind people who were friends of her parents. She visited them often when she traveled to Florida to see her parents. And she had worked as an assistant for seven years to a man who became deaf from cannonball explosions in World War II. He didn't sign, but read lips. The Riedels thought Andrea would fit the job well, so she became Bert's companion and support person.

Uneasy at first, Andrea felt herself in one world while Bert seemed to be in another—a world that only touched the periphery of hers. She'd close her eyes and try to shut out sound in an effort to put herself where he was. In time, as she watched Bert move carefully and confidently throughout the house, Andrea became more comfortable with Bert. She saw that he trusted her without reservation to protect him. She in turn committed to always be alert and diligent for him.

That diligence included leaping into sign language study so she could communicate better with Bert. Once a week, after her shift with him, she and I worked to expand her sign vocabulary. Because Bert had difficulty reading her left-handed fingerspelling, she practiced spelling with both hands until she could spell comfortably with her right hand. In spite of my reassurance to her that Bert would eventually adapt to her left-handed signing, Andrea became proficient at right-handed fingerspelling. As she and Bert spent many hours in each other's company, her spunky personality melded perfectly with his. They established their own way of communicating. Andrea used the limited signs she knew and depended on pointing, taps, and gestures for everything else she needed to say when they weren't at the braille machine.

The two made quite a pair. Though not a big man, Bert was nearly a head taller than Andrea. His white hair contrasted with her bob of dark curls. When they strolled together along the path circling Evergreen Lake, she pressed her forearm against his, locking it tight against her body. With that safeguard against the slightest teeter, she would lead their pace. Invariably, she'd swing her arm and it would set off a song in Bert's head. As she sang along, their steps slid into its rhythm. Bert heard her through the tempo of her step and in "Yankee Doodle Dandy" as she tapped in rhythm on his cap, singing, "stuck a feather in his hat and called it macaroni." Even with four decades between them, they knew many of the same tunes. They enjoyed their time in the sun, imitating Dinah Shore singing, "See the U.S.A in your Chevrolet."

Sometimes they walked on the road near the house. Once while they walked, Andrea shut her eyes for a moment to discern her environment through smell, as Bert did. When she quickly detected the aroma of popcorn, she determined (as did Bert) that the wafting scent came from the house next door.

At the Riedels' home, if John and Mary were out, Andrea prepared Bert's meals. When she ate with him, she closed her eyes sometimes to find that ordinary food suddenly became superbly delicious. Bert liked it when she made his favorite dish—a bowl of stewed tomatoes and asparagus on toast. "For my last meal on earth," he told her, "I want stewed tomatoes and asparagus on toast."

Working at Bert's desk, Andrea used his new computer to transpose his correspondence into braille, and she taught Bert how to use the computer. With braille letters on two keys marking where to place his hands, she showed him how to use a light touch to keep from dragging the letters. Eventually Bert gave up his old manual Olympia typewriter and used the computer to compose letters and write poetry.

Andrea watched Bert as he imprinted each line of poetry to memory, mindful of the amount of energy it required. Because Bert couldn't see his own typing, he had to memorize his poems before he typed them into the computer. Andrea proofread and corrected his typing. Then she transposed the poems into braille so he could read and refine them if he wished. Sometimes she typed the poems as he recited them to her.

While she worked on his correspondence, Andrea listened to Bert play the piano. Married to a professional musician, she shared Bert's appreciation for music. She breathed the music along with him. She admired how Bert played with refined style, pausing to lift his hands most beautifully like a dancer, then set them down again on the last chord. His foot on the pedal resonated the finale.

While she perceived the beauty of Bert's music through her ears, she knew he depended on the vibrations, hearing only glimmers of notes now and then. His hearing aid lent him only security, as he picked up intermittent hints of his favorite sonatas. He played the pieces anyway, for hours some days. And just when Andrea thought she knew his whole repertoire of classical and whimsical ditties, he surprised her with others.

Along with enjoying Bert's gift of music, Andrea respected his well-maintained competitive edge at honeymoon bridge. She had to hone up quickly to be a match for him. She made time for the card games that usually brought out the rowdy side in both of them. In other more thought-provoking times, the two uncovered their philosophical views in more serious discussions.

"When I go," Bert said, "I want to leave with a smile on my face and go back to the earth to make other things grow." He explained his philosophy in more detail. "Life's transcendental. Helen raised our children with a true sense of love and understanding. They emulate her, and now she lives on in them in a transcendental way."

Andrea contributed much to their conversations. The only thing handicapping her was the machine that cramped the steady flow of her thoughts that had to be typed out. There was simply never enough time to say them all.

Swimming became another of Bert and Andrea's regular activities. It was a twenty-four-mile round-trip to the Evergreen Recreation Center. Various volunteers had driven Bert to the pool before Andrea. A couple of times I had taken Bert there myself. We would divert from our normal routine of sign language lessons and head off to the pool instead.

One day during our ride over to the pool, Bert talked about the stock market and politics. Every once in a while he asked me a question that I tried to answer with fingerspelling. It was hard for him to read my signs when we were seated side by side in the car. It required some gymnastics for me to steer with my left hand and sign with my right, while manipulating a stick shift. My shoulder twisted back awkwardly when I offered him my hand. It was unnatural for us both, so it took him a long time to read even one word. The stoplights along the route were few and weren't long enough for him to read my fingerspelling. Consequently, most of my conversation was reduced to a few *yes* and *no* taps and some half-spelled words. It couldn't have been very interesting for him—the logistics of the situation made me a boring conversationalist. Bert talked on anyway. I guessed he was used to conversations where his listener drifted off like that. Somehow the discussion turned to the topic of "nature versus nurture" as related to character building.

"What makes one child in a family become successful, I wonder, while others in the same family never amount to anything?" he asked, over the drone of the motor.

I didn't know if this was meant to be a rhetorical question but felt compelled to answer it anyway. "T-h-e-y are born that way."

"They're born that way," Bert repeated as he translated out loud. He contemplated my response for a second. "Yes, I guess so," he said.

I smiled feeling a swell of pride, not because he agreed with me, but because he understood my signing on the first try—while I was driving. In the parking lot I pulled into a handicapped space near the building's entrance. Mary had lent me a handicapped parking tag to hang on the mirror.

Bert felt the car stop. "Are we here already?" he asked.

"Yes." I tapped his leg twice before stepping out of and around the car to help him out. A few raindrops hit my bare legs as the breeze kicked up. The dark clouds overhead looked ready to dump on us any minute. Bert felt the weather change, too. "It's raining," he said with a delighted chuckle.

"I-not-have-umbrella. You-me-need-run," I joked.

Bert laughed heartily. "The rain won't hurt. We're just going to get wet anyway." He carried his own athletic bag over his shoulder—his "valise," he called it—and held my arm as I surveyed whether to walk him the longer way using the handicap ramp or the shorter way up the three steps at the front of the building. I decided on the ramp. A string of yellow school buses parked at the end of the ramp spewed exhaust where we started up the incline. The smell triggered a flashback to my former job as a day camp director.

Bert interrupted my thoughts. "Where're we going?" he asked. "We're going uphill. This is a different way." John must have usually led him up the front steps. Grasping my arm a little tighter Bert laughed again and started to sing. He bounced next to me with every step, enjoying the mood of his song as the raindrops plopped down around us. Then the doors to the building flung open, spilling out a stream of kids in full flight running toward the buses. They ran right past us, oblivious to me and the singing old man.

I mused at the poignancy of the scene—it was such a contrast between where I had been and where I was now. Not too many years ago, I was in charge of kids just like them, fifty of them, in perpetual high gear, running to get on buses. That was in Denver. Now I was in Evergreen, in charge of one, deaf-blind, eighty-seven-year-old. Both jobs had bountiful challenges and rewards.

Inside the lobby of the recreation center, I led Bert to the left, to the small private restroom, as John had instructed me. Bert could maneuver independently in there to change his clothes, instead of in the men's locker room. The staff at the Evergreen Recreation Center were well acquainted with Bert and they accommodated his special needs by assigning him a private lane in the pool where he wouldn't tangle up with other swimmers. He relied on the wall and the lane rope to guide himself as he swam the length of the pool. This day, however, turned out to be "kids day" for the summer day camp. There were no ropes blocking off lanes for adult lap swimmers. The other eighty kids from the day camp who didn't get on the buses were all in the pool, and the lifeguards explained they couldn't put up a lane rope just for Bert.

"It's no problem," I told them. "We can handle a few kids." I'd been a swimming instructor before and had years of experience with kids. I could just swim alongside Bert. I knew he loved his weekly pool exercise and I didn't want to deny him that just because some kids were in the pool.

Bert emerged from his private changing area wearing his printed Speedo tank suit, green flip-flops, and a neon yellow swim cap. He stood with his valise and white cane, waiting for me to lead him to the pool. I was surprised to see him in such snazzy swimming attire.

The warm, humid air and scent of chlorine enveloped us as we entered the pool area. He wanted to put his valise and cane on the bleachers before I walked him over to the edge of the pool. I decided to warn him of the situation with the day camp and the multitude of kids in the pool. "Many, many children are in pool," I signed. "You do not have l-a-n-e."

"The kids are here. That's okay," Bert said. He was always accommodating. Still, I knew he had no idea about what a circus it was in there. I guided him to the ladder, placing his hand onto the smooth and shiny chrome so he could lower himself into the water. I followed him into the pool, jumping up and down on my tiptoes until I got used to the cold water. Bert didn't seem to notice the chilly temperature as he began his twenty lengths.

He took four breaststrokes with his face down, raised his head for a mouthful of air, and continued in the same pattern down the length of the pool. I swam close-by, with frequent touches to his arm to let him know I was there. Bert had been a lifeguard on the Chicago beaches of Lake Michigan and always spoke with joy about swimming. Next to music and bridge, I knew this was his favorite pastime.

"I've loved swimming ever since I was a little boy," Bert had said. "I remember clearly, seeing my grandfather's bald head as he swam far out into the lake. I was so impressed with him that I always wanted to swim like that." Bert spoke with pride about teaching his son Philip to swim at the lakes in Maine. He beamed, remembering his daughter Sue, doing her pretty dives. I continued to swim close to Bert. For both his and the unassuming children's safety, I was his eyes and ears. Every time a youngster swam in his path, I warned them, "He can't see you, he's blind."

"He is?" they asked. "How can he swim?"

"He just does," I said. "And he can't hear either."

"Really?" they said. They would break from their splashing for a second to consider this and then continue with their water play. Suddenly, five or six boys about eight years old came running out of the locker room toward the pool. I cringed, knowing they were going to jump in at the five-foot mark, right in front of Bert.

"Wait!" I yelled. "He can't see you—he's blind." I had to repeat this for every kid because each one's attention was on something different. One by one they stopped to look at the swimmer who couldn't see them. "He can't hear you either," I said. "He's deaf." By then, I had everyone's attention and they sat down, lining the edge of the pool. With the immediate danger gone, it became funny watching their faces with dumbfounded expressions. In unison, they watched the yellow cap float by them down to the deep end and turn back. Their unleashed excitement was abandoned for a few moments as they sat stunned, in disbelief that someone deaf and blind could actually swim. When their curiosity was satisfied, they jumped back into the pool and I resumed my warnings to other unassuming swimmers.

Finally Bert sensed that our situation was a little precarious with all the kids splashing around. "I think I've had enough for today," he said. "I did ten laps. We'll come back another day." Though I felt badly that his swim had been cut short, I was relieved that no one jumped in on top of him or banged heads with him. Bert never complained about the kids or that he didn't get to finish his twenty laps.

A week or so after our eventful swim day, Andrea accompanied Bert and me to the pool so that I could familiarize her with the swimming routine. Everything went without a hitch and afterward we stopped at a near-by Baskin Robbins for ice cream. "Shall I just run in and get him a cone?" Andrea offered.

"No, let's go in," I said. Now that Bert had a vehicle for communication, I was eager to expose him to some of the wonders of the day—thirty-one flavors of ice cream. Who knew if he had ever seen more than three? With Bert's hand on my arm, I perused the double row of ice-cream buckets sitting behind the glass counters. A young girl in a baseball cap had the job of scooping up cones. She glanced up at us as I was signing to Bert, "T-h-e-y have many, many f-l-a—"

"I'll have chocolate," Bert said.

There were cherries jubilee, pralines 'n cream, baseball nut, pistachio almond, coconut fudge, pink bubblegum, daiquiri ice, and more. Surely, Bert would like to know them. I started again. "T-h-e-y have p-r-a-l-i-n-e—"

"Praline?" he questioned, pronouncing it with a long *i* like *line*. "I'll have chocolate."

I looked at the girl in the baseball cap. She was watching us and patiently waiting with her arms folded on top of the counter. "Um . . ." I said, slowly resigning my enthusiasm for all the flavors, "he'll have chocolate."

Andrea paid for Bert's cone and the three of us sat at a tiny table for two. While she tended to Bert's melting dribbles of chocolate with a napkin, we joked and chatted. Andrea took over the swimming outings from then on. I resumed my role as sign language teacher.

Growing Pains

Toward the end of summer, Mary moved us downstairs to Bert's apartment for our lessons—away from the center of activity in the kitchen. The big windows downstairs gave me the feeling we were sitting among the butterflies in the meadow outside. A four-foot-sized wedding picture of Bert and Helen hung across from our work table. Each time I sat with Bert, I looked over at Helen. It was as though she were right there with us.

The power brailler remained upstairs at the kitchen table. Bert's proficiency with sign language had increased to the point where I could manage our lessons without it. This change, we decided, was like moving on to high school, even though our communication was still rather basic and slow-going.

Shortly after our move downstairs, Bert began a session excitedly describing a hike his daughter, Marcia, took with Mary and John. "They trekked thirteen thousand feet up to the Navajo Peak. It's on the Continental Divide, south of Rocky Mountain National Park. Marcia saw a one-million-year-old rock that left her feeling a primal connection with civilization. I wish I could see it," he said.

"I wish I could see it, too." I signed. I figured Marcia or John had brailled the description of their hike for him.

"I refuse to think about passing away," Bert interjected. "I have goals for myself. I want to live! I still have a lot of things to do. Learning. Learning is the key. I want to learn the computer and I want to master sign language, though I'll never be as good as you are," he chuckled.

Adventures like his kids' Navajo Peak climb always got Bert reflecting on his own life's adventures. Bert frequently started our lessons this way—with a warm greeting, and then like an erupting dam, he burst forth with whatever was on his mind. Usually, he inserted some positive or important message about life. While I listened, I would organize my papers and set my mind on a direction for the day's lesson. I liked to share what was happening in my life, too. Our informal conversation exercised his brain and was a good warm-up for reading sign language. It provided him with one more connection to the world he missed.

Knowing it takes about forty exposures to a word before a person can incorporate it into their vocabulary, I'd repeat signs with Bert that we covered the week before, slipping them into our conversation. Repetition was even more important for Bert because he was elderly. With whatever time was remaining in our session, I worked on building new sign vocabulary or lessons in ASL grammar. Some days we discussed or clarified something someone had said that confused him or we hashed over something that was bothering him.

As we worked, Bert sometimes added words into his interpretations, words I didn't sign. This led him way off track, and it could take fifteen minutes to clear up a misunderstanding. My mind would race to a better solution, and it was a strain not to switch to a different approach when our communication moved slowly. But Bert taught me something about patience. Switching gears midstream was not wise. He methodically held onto the train of thought as we worked through a sentence, stumbling over signs. Many times, when I thought I totally confused him, when I almost forgot what I'd been trying to say in the first place, Bert would bring the conversation back around to exactly what I meant.

One day I was signing, "You are reading sign language well now." He interpreted this as, "You are reading about sign language."

"I d-i-d not say the word *a-b-o-u-t*," I told him. "I d-i-d say that you are reading my sign language."

He didn't follow what I meant. He wasn't familiar with the terminology *to read sign language*. He couldn't see where he'd gotten off track and repeatedly inserted the word *about*. With a wrinkled expression, he looked hurt or upset, as though I were playing a mean trick. Then he inserted the word *talk* for *sign* and started guessing all kinds of interpretations.

"Noooo," I said, frustrated, tapping him once. He kept guessing words—not even understanding the one tap for *no*. I needed to halt the confusion. I took his hands and placed them on both sides of my head, shaking it from side to side.

"No?" he asked. My antics broke the tension that was starting to build and he sat back in his chair and started laughing. I started laughing, too. I took a deep breath and we started over. He persevered, staying with me while I varied my approach.

"You can understand sign language very good now," I signed. This time he got it.

A tendency among people who can hear is to drop something that isn't working, move onto something else, or change the subject completely. It doesn't work that way with deaf-blind people. They don't change subjects so readily as hearing people do. They lack the visual and auditory cues that indicate these transitions. Without clear transitions the confusion compounds.

Bert's habit of putting unwanted words into our sentences had John, Mary, and I grappling with ways to deal with that. I had to think up a signal that wouldn't get confused with a sign but would alert Bert to when he had misinterpreted. I came up with a strategy that proved to be a huge time-saver. We taught Bert that when we pressed on the inside of his right forearm with our index finger, it meant he had wrongly interpreted a word. From then on, he knew immediately when he was off-track. We'd start over with a fresh slate instead of getting tangled in a mass of confusion.

Some of my frustration was due to the process of weaning us off of the braille machine. These were our "growing pains" as Bert began to internalize the language. Yet the frustrations soon turned into rewards because Bert was able to hold onto a train of thought and think it through until it made sense. I never saw Bert give up or quit trying to understand. He had the strong desire to succeed. He understood a bit more every day and was beginning to see how the puzzle pieces of sign fit together.

Senses

Bert was at his downstairs piano when I arrived from the sweltering city. While he played Franz Liszt's "Liebestraume," I settled into the wooden chair in his apartment. My shirt, still wet from perspiration during the commute, clung to my back. The sweat on the back of my thighs made them stick to the seat. Thankful for the coolness of the apartment, I reached for the spiral notebook Jean Kelly and I kept at the table. We shared a log of our lessons with Bert to reinforce each other's work. I didn't get to see Jean much, so the notebook kept us connected and moving in the same direction. We gave each other encouragement and support in our notes and sometimes shared funny things that came up in the lessons. We even talked a bit about our kids.

I liked her drawings of hands making signs and the clouds she drew around her questions: "Is that how you do it?" she would write. Jean drew pictures of herself with frazzled expressions. I got a kick out of how she described Bert misinterpreting the sign she made for *thoughts* as *crazy*. She wrote: "thoughts—index finger circling at temple—He kept saying 'cuckoo.' Maybe I'm the one who's cuckoo." Other times she would let me know how her lesson with Bert went: "He's reading signs great today," or "Phew, this is hard work." Bert didn't know what we wrote in our notes. Nevertheless, the logbook came to be a treasured link between the three of us.

Bert continued to play as I finished reviewing her
notes. When he came to the end of the piece, he paused.
"Okay, I think that's enough," he said aloud to himself. He
lifted the crystal on his watch and touched the silver metal
hands inside. "Three o'clock," he announced, closing the
glass cover. He leaned down and felt for the cane at his
feet before scooting to the end of the bench. He rocked a
few times and pushed himself up with a "here we go." A
pink sunburn on his cheeks and the green camp shorts he
wore gave testimony to an earlier walk on his path.

Until now, I'd only seen Bert in jeans or corduroys.
"Hello," I called. Heading toward me, he stopped for a second as if listening, then took a few more steps. "Hi, Bert," I
called again, on the off chance that he might pick up the
sound of my voice. He didn't respond. I often used my
voice when I signed with him. I didn't expect him to hear
me—he never seemed to, but I'd seen him react to other
people's laughing or occasional noises, like the ringing of
my cell phone. I wanted to give him the benefit of the
doubt. After a few more steps, when his cane met the back
of a chair, I stood to greet him. He startled at my touch and
broke into a smile. He was expecting me.

"How *are* you?" he said, giving me a tight hug.

I was eager to ask Bert a question. Because he'd had
sight for the first half of his life, I wanted to know if he was
able to visualize sign language—see the signs on my hands
moving through the air. As soon as we sat down, I asked him.

"No," he said, "I feel them with my hands."

I hadn't expected this answer because he often
described his memories visually and with such pleasure,
like how he remembered young Marcia's pigtails flopping
up and down as she jumped in the leaves. I was disappointed. Sign language was so beautiful. I wanted him to

"see" it—even if it was only in his mind. My disappointment carried through the rest of our lesson.

Days later, however, I began to develop a new appreciation of Bert's method of seeing after reading what neurologist Oliver Sacks wrote about seeing by touch. In his 1995 book, *An Anthropologist on Mars*, Sacks described a fifty-year-old blind patient named Virgil who suffered from poor eyesight as a toddler and, after illnesses and a cataract at age six, became totally blind. Despite his blindness, Virgil made a good life for himself, holding a job as an adult. Later, after forty-five years of blindness, he underwent restorative surgery for his vision.

Subsequently, Virgil suffered from great confusion because his brain had no idea how to interpret the new cacophony of light, color, and movement his eyes were seeing. Virgil had difficulty distinguishing his cat from his dog until he could touch them. Shapes required strenuous visual retraining. Colors were easier to grasp. In a grocery store, the sea of visual stimuli was overwhelming. "Everything ran together,"[16] he said.

Virgil found walking without his cane "scary" and "confusing" because he wasn't able to judge distance and space. He could pick out only parts of objects, not their whole. It was difficult to determine whether Virgil's problems were physiological or psychological.

In time, some of Virgil's vision problems improved, indicating he would eventually accommodate to his new vision. Still, touch remained his preferred mode for interpreting his environment. The concentration required for him to see with his eyes was simply too fatiguing. His eyes were functioning, yet he continued his blind habits and behaviors, seeing the world the way he was accustomed. He wasn't like a cataract patient who remembers how to interpret images after the cataract is removed.

Oliver Sacks referred to other blind patients studied by Alberto Valvo, an Italian ophthalmologist. Valvo wrote about his patients' difficulties in adjusting to changes in their cerebral functioning after sight restoration. Along with the tremendous expenditure of energy required for their brains to interpret new sight impressions, his patients were trying to handle new expectations from others who did not understand that it takes time to learn how to see. Adding to the stress of coping with these demands was their disappointment that objects didn't appear as they had them pictured in their minds. Sadness occurred, as well, with realizing how much they'd missed during their blind years. The patients fell into depression.

One of Valvo's patients, "H. S.," became blind by a chemical explosion at age fifteen. Twenty-two years later, H. S. had his sight restored by a corneal transplant but was left with no distance or depth perception. He became terrified of things like traffic, and he experienced more fear than he had when he was blind. Reading presented challenges, too, as initially he was only able to make out individual letters. He couldn't scan through whole words. H. S. expressed the difficult adjustment as "too long and unhappy a road, leading one into a strange world."[17] Describing these phases of rehabilitation, Valvo wrote, "Patients in this depressive stage return often to using the sense of touch."[18]

Learning to see after blindness requires a dramatic shift in neurological functioning just as it does in learning to perceive after the onset of blindness. At first, blindness is a devastating loss, but with time the mind reorients and adapts. Bert had adapted to his blindness, yet with his visual memory I thought he'd be more like the cataract patient and be able to visualize sign language. But after forty-five years of blindness, he could not. He saw sign language with his hands, much like he read using his fingers.[19]

Just as it takes time to learn how to see, it also takes time to learn how to hear. Barbie Galoob, a good friend of mine, after more than forty years of deafness, had a cochlear implant operation (electrodes placed into the inner ear) that gave her partial hearing. Barbie shared some of her journal entries with family and friends, describing what it was like during the two months after the "hook up" of her implant.

At first "all the sounds were alike," Barbie wrote. "Water running, telephone rings and children's yells. But now I can identify sounds by different patterns." While walking her dogs, Barbie discovered how noisy fall leaves are when her dogs went sniffing among them. She heard ocean waves while vacationing with her family. And there was another sound that continued for a long time. When she asked her nephew who was nearby what the noise was, he replied, "Birds chirping." Barbie had never realized how birds sounded. She wrote, "To tell you honestly, it was very loud and annoying, but it was the very first time for me to hear them singing and I'm sure they will begin to sound beautiful." Another time, Barbie thought she was hearing an airplane, which turned out to be a vacuum cleaner.

At a restaurant, Barbie listened to an annoying noise repeatedly for almost two hours. She thought the noise came from a meat-cutting machine or perhaps from an ice machine. Finally, when the lunch rush subsided, she asked a waitress as to the origin of the puzzling noise. The waitress didn't understand her, so Barbie wrote the question on a napkin, explaining briefly about her new cochlear implant and that sounds were new to her. The waitress read the note, made a face, and simply pointed to a speaker in the ceiling. Barbie reacted by saying, "You mean music or talk from the loudspeaker?" The waitress merely nodded and asked if she wanted the volume turned down. Barbie shook her head and thanked the waitress, feeling much better just knowing where the sound was coming from.

Several days later at a different restaurant, Barbie heard a noise similar to what she'd heard at the first restaurant—a noise she thought, again, sounded like a meat machine. Turning to her kids, she asked what it was. They replied that it was music from the loudspeaker. "I couldn't believe how loud it was and I felt sorry for the hearing people who have to listen to constant noise," she wrote.

Although Barbie didn't initially like the noises she experienced, over time my friend grew to love her new hearing, especially hearing music. However, since the first implants in 1961, until well after their approval by the Food and Drug Administration in 1984, cochlear implants have been a controversial subject in the Deaf Community. Some recipients of the earliest technology, unsatisfied with the noise, disabled their devices, preferring the quiet they'd known instead. Others in the Deaf Community opposed implants (and some still do), resisting the hearing community's push to "make" them hearing. Some have not forgotten the past when oralism prevailed and educators forced them to lipread and to speak. They are reminded of their anger and frustration in trying to understand and produce speech. Today, comfortable with their deafness and proud of their language of ASL, they're worried about how implants will affect the younger deaf generation. They don't want anything, including implants, to take the place of their beautiful visual language and their Deaf Culture.

With improved technology, some attitudes are changing. Deaf children are receiving enormous benefits from the devices, and adults who have lost hearing later in life are enjoying their restored hearing. Their brains are already familiar with what sounds are, so they adapt more easily to the new sounds they receive from the implant.

• • • • •

Bert's family, concerned about preserving his quality of life, had investigated procedures to restore his eyesight as well as his hearing. He'd had an evaluation in the late 1980s that showed that the retinal nerve was destroyed, obliterating the possibility of saving his vision. The same level of hope regarding his hearing was eliminated in 1995 when experts at Stanford University concluded that Bert had irreversible auditory nerve damage. A cochlear implant would not have restored sound resolution. Resigned to the gradual losses, Bert adapted over time and gained value from his other senses.

Being with Bert gave me a new perspective on how I tune into my senses. Though my ears pick up sounds, I don't hear them unless I'm listening. The television may be on, but I don't hear it if I'm busy reading. Even when my eyes perceive someone walking by, I won't see the person if I'm intently listening to the radio. With all my senses intact, I seem to focus on one at a time. I trust the other senses and they alert me when I suddenly need to pay attention to something else.

But aren't our senses more complicated than simply seeing, tasting, or smelling? What about intuition, impressions, and emotions? Are these not part of our sensory input process? Using visual and auditory cues, we're able to perceive a great deal more information and understanding from a speaker's words. Without these cues Bert was at a double disadvantage. He had the braille machine, but it was monotone. He had sign language, but even that didn't convey nuances of subtle tones in voices and semaphores of facial muscles. How could he perceive the worried looks, the welcoming smiles, the eager anticipation, the sadness, the impatience, the discomfort, the puzzlement, or the wonder of those in his midst?

Since toddlerhood, Helen Keller had developed a mental acuity from which she gleaned nearly the same information about her environment as sighted and hearing people. She could detect subtle variations in people's muscular movements and discern their mental as well as emotional states. She could recognize impatience in jerking motions or approval in a pat. She felt affection in soft touches and sensed a command in a firm gesture. She could detect fear by a brusque change in someone's behavior. Helen distinguished flowers by their individual scents and even recognized people in the same manner.

Because Bert was not born blind and deaf, I wondered if his acuity was as sharp as Helen's, especially since he told me he felt the signs with his hands. I contemplated how Bert perceived his world and the people around him—how he interpreted his environment. I brought the subject up during a lesson as we sat outside his apartment one day. As we talked about what was on my mind, I asked him, "How do you know when people are laughing?"

"I don't know," he said. "Some people don't change their movement much. I laugh when I think it's appropriate. I don't always know if they're laughing unless I can feel their motion. But I get a sense from how they touch me if they're comfortable with me."

Bert grew more reflective. "Sometimes people know me, but I don't ever know them. I'm an old man now. I've seen a lot of life. I watched my children grow up. I can sense attitude and gratitude. Since you can't see the soul or the bottom of the heart, you have to become a master of understanding. You see if people follow through with their commitments. Some people are only nice for the occasion. If their commitments hold up, then you can detect what's in their mind and in their heart. It's all about appreciation," he said.

"You see with your s-o-u-l," I signed.

"That's it," Bert said. He finished his train of thought. "I just want to be nice to people. I have enough problems without problems in relationships."

Bert used his intuition well and he made maximum use of his physical senses. He had a prominent sense of smell and was sensitive to cleanliness. He could tell who smoked and who didn't, who had bathed and who hadn't. He could identify a specific woman by her perfume and could tell which room in the house was the bedroom by its smell. "Bedrooms usually have stale air. The air gets musty from breathing and movement. I like to open my windows several times a day and just take some deep breaths," he said. "I'm sensitive to heat and cold, although I don't jump up and stumble over things to turn the thermostat up and down. Sighted people can do that easily in seconds. It might take me ten minutes," he chuckled. Bert was patient with his environment. "I know it will change in a little while anyway," he added.

"How do you know if it's cloudy or sunny?" I asked.

"You usually get wind with the clouds. With the sun, there's a hint of warmth on your face and the light hits the eyes just a bit. I love wind." His eyes opened wide and a smile broke out as if he was anticipating a breeze right then. "It's invigorating. I wrote a poem about it called 'My Friend the Wind.'" Bert recited the poem for me about the different moods of the wind: its tender soft touching on his face to its monumental blows and how it takes time to visit him while it spreads life-bearing seeds to all corners of the earth.

Bert used his sense of touch to experience the environment. He used touch to feel his physical surroundings and to interpret my body language and my sign language. He knew me pretty well after more than a year of lessons. From everyday hello and good-bye hugs, he knew my height was about the same as his and that I was on the slim side, but I was faceless. Wasn't he curious to know what his friends looked like? Did he care that I had brown eyes and shoulder-length brown hair with natural highlights?

"Do you know what I look like?" I asked. "Do you want to feel my face?" I brought his hands up to my cheeks inviting him. Politely, Bert felt the curves of my cheekbones and my jaw line. With the appreciation of a dentist, my lips and straight teeth impressed him most.

"Nice, symmetrical features," he said, "though I don't care much about physical beauty," he confessed. "I always wondered why Helen Keller was feeling faces. Does that really say if they are beautiful or ugly?"

"She did feel faces, though mostly she was reading their lips with her fingers. It's called t-a-d-o-m-a." I put his fingers on my lips and continued talking to give him the idea.

"I can't imagine that. That's too hard," he said. "I could never read lips like that. I'm not interested in feeling faces. I'm more interested in the substance of someone's personality and intellect. I prefer interesting interaction and mental stimulation. That's how I judge beauty."

A Visual Symphony

For several months I'd been mulling over whether to introduce Bert to American Sign Language. Up until now we'd been conversing using Signed English. Hearing people who are beginners in sign language tend to gravitate toward Signed English because it follows the English word order—a sign can be used for each English word as it is spoken. ASL, however, is the sign language most preferred by an estimated 500,000 users in the Deaf Community.[20] Rich with expression it contains all the essential elements of a complete language without using English word order.

I'd already introduced John and Mary to some ASL principles so that they'd be prepared when they encountered ASL users in the community. For Bert, who was not out in the mainstream, I pondered over the pros and cons of introducing another level of complexity.

Although I wanted Bert to have an awareness of this natural language of the deaf, which can oftentimes express a thought more interestingly and succinctly than we can in Signed English, I had some concerns. First was the issue of facial expression, which is so crucial to the meaning of the message in ASL but was useless to Bert. A head shake from side to side signed with a statement negates it. Bert would miss the head shake and therefore misinterpret the statement. If a snooty facial expression of the signer accompanied an action sign like *walk,* for example, Bert would not know that the signer was describing a "disgruntled" person walking. There are other facial markers, like raised eyebrows, meaning the speaker is asking a *yes* or *no* question, that Bert also would not be able to grasp. These elements of ASL were effective with sighted users, though ineffective with Bert.

And there was the issue of tenses. Time signs, like *yesterday* or *tomorrow,* usually come at the beginning of a sentence, to let the listener know the time period being referred to. But the sign *finish,* which often comes at the end of a sentence, means something has been completed. A beginner could easily get confused.

Time is not always specified in ASL but rather referred to in nuances of movement that can be so subtle one can miss them. Signing close to the body usually represents the present, and signs made slightly pulled back either toward or behind the body may signify something that happened in the past. Signing further out from the body may indicate something happening in the future. To fluent sign language users, understanding these nuances is easy, just as it is for English users to understand the subtleties of English—words in sentences that trip up foreigners or deaf persons who are trying to learn the language, such as: *The bandage was wound around the wound.* Or *The farm was used to produce produce,* or *There is no time like the present to present the present.*

Although some elements of ASL would confound Bert, there were others I thought he'd enjoy very much. Signs placed in various locations in space coupled with changes in movement, speed, and direction would give Bert interesting and fun pictorial information that Signed

English could not. ASL is like painting pictures in the air with dancing hands. It is art just as music and poetry are.

Bert loved poetry, and I wanted to show him how we could put his poetry onto our hands. But first he would have to understand something about ASL. We'd come so far already. I'd seen him blossom more with everything offered to him. Why should I decide what limits Bert should have?

So I prepared a lesson on ASL. I began it with Bert by typing into the brailler, which fortuitously had made its way downstairs. I hadn't asked Mary for the machine, but this complex lesson would have been a bear without it.

"American Sign Language, or ASL, is made up of words," I started. The next part I signed into Bert's hands. "Words are made of four things."

"Four things," he repeated.

That part was easy. He embedded four seeds in his mind, preparing for what was coming next.

"The first e-l-e-m-e-n-t is h-a-n-d-s-h-a-p-e."

"Handshake," he interpreted.

"No, h-a-n-d-s-h-a-p-e."

"Oh, *shape*, I see."

"Yes, like the letters *f, c,* and *b*. The next two elements are l-o-c-a-t-i-o-n and m-o-v-e-m-e-n-t," I taught. "Like *family*. You place your hands in front of your body, both hands in the *f* handshape with palms facing out. As they each circle outward they meet with their palms facing in." Next, I illustrated *drink* using the *c* handshape in the gesture of bringing a cup to the mouth, and then *book,* with my flat palms facing up. When they opened and shut, they emulated the covers of a book opening.

Bert followed along with me, moving his hands back and forth from my hands to the braille machine, repeating my words out loud.

"And the fourth is p-a-l-m o-r-i-e-n-t-a-t-i-o-n," I signed.

"Or—what?" he asked. "I didn't get that."

This is cruel, I thought. I hated to give him long words. He rarely got them. Resting my elbow on my knee with my hand straight up I started to respell *orientation*. My heel rose from the floor when my toes pushed down against the weight of my signing arm. Slowly, he read each letter as I felt my foot going to sleep.

"O-r-i-e-n—, Oriental," he announced quickly.

"No," I said, with one tap. I went back to the brailler. Even on the brailler, it took him a few tries to get the word. "Palm orientation. It refers to which way your palm is facing."

I explained two more characteristics of ASL, *repetition* and *directionality*. "If you repeat the sign *go* several times, moving it in a different direction each time, you create the word *errands*. If you repeat the same sign *go* several times in the same place, it means *to go there regularly*." We practiced with simple stories in ASL about where he goes regularly and that Mary goes on errands. Last, I used Signed English to tell the same stories so he could understand the difference. Bert interpreted the stories as I signed them and then he signed them back to me. The lesson on the elements of ASL for John and Mary took one hour. Bert and I needed about eight sessions to cover the same material, but he absorbed every ounce of it.

A week after introducing Bert to ASL, I got goose bumps when Andrea, Bert's companion, reported to me that Bert had taught *her* the elements of ASL. She recited them imitating Bert's voice: "*Handshape, location, movement,* and *palm orientation*." Bert hadn't left out the other two characteristics of ASL either: *repetition* and *directionality*.

• • • • •

It would not be until after much practice, when Bert was more comfortable with sign language, that we actually enjoyed some ASL poetry together. I introduced Lou Fant's poem, "The Watercycle." Lou Fant was a hearing child of deaf parents and a brilliant interpreter. As an educator and founding member of the National Theater of the Deaf, Fant was said to have been able to make passages from the phone book sing like poetry because of his extraordinary gift using ASL.[21] Fant was known for his creation of poetry in ASL. In "The Watercycle," the scenes were most powerful because they were depicted using variations of only one handshape (the number five) flowing one into the other.

Although I never had the opportunity to see Lou Fant perform his poem, I learned it from how he portrayed it in a book and I showed it to Bert. First I described it on the braille machine: "Clouds building until they break into a light rain. They turn into a heavy downpour. The water flows into rivulets that grow into a raging river of rapids that spill over a waterfall into a whirling vortex. The water eventually flows out to sea, where it becomes little ocean waves that change into big ocean waves. The waves change into wind and evaporate and then become clouds."

I performed the poem for Bert with my hands, bending and wiggling my fingers, as I imagined Lou Fant's hands, flowing like water. Through a circle of space, the poem ended in the same place where it began.[22]

Fant's poem was a visual symphony. Bert loved it. His face lit up when I signed it. I didn't realize how much Bert loved it until I returned the next time and he performed it back to me. He had memorized it.

I Can Hear the Words in My Head

The hand of the blind man goes with him as an eye to his work and by its silent reading with finger on the raised page shortens his long hours of ennui. It ministers as willingly to the deaf, educates them, and if they cannot speak, its fingers speak words of cheer to their eye, which thus becomes an ear.

—HELEN KELLER, *Magic in Your Fingers*

Each time I arrived at the Riedels' and went down the stairs, I was delighted to find Bert waiting for me in his sitting room. One day, in early September, I was especially touched to find *he* had arranged our chairs in the way I liked—facing each other. The braille machine forever rested on the table at his side. Usually he was reading his braille copy of the *New York Times* or *National Geographic* magazine. This day I found him practicing signing by himself. It stopped me dead in my tracks before announcing myself. Instead, I stood listening for a moment, smiling while he talked his awkward fingers through their new way of communication.

When I finally tapped his arm, he jumped with a start. "Ah!" he said. With each visit, I always tried tapping more gently, hoping to avoid startling him. He startled anyway, and his fingers would suddenly be off the dotted page if he was reading. He'd say, "Who is it?" at the same time bending down the corner of the page to mark his spot.

Today he asked, "Is this Diane?" As usual, his blue eyes stared off into space, but his expression livened when I offered him my hand in the shape of the letter *d*. With his question answered and confirmed, he pushed himself up from the chair. "How are you?" Bert's characteristically warm greeting made me smile and feel newly special each time I saw him.

"GREAT," I signed, before he gave me a big hug. We had barely sat down before he began talking about some of his everyday struggles with deaf-blindness.

"You know, being blind and deaf requires more concentration and expenditure of energy to do even the simplest things. I have to crystallize information in my memory because I can't save papers with little notes to refresh my memory," he said. "Sometimes I forget things. I forget about latitude and longitude and I don't know where I am. 'Is this the bathroom?' I ask myself."

I'd seen Bert take wrong turns in the house before. In spite of his keen memory of the number of steps required to find the piano, if any distracting thoughts disturbed his concentration, he'd find himself in the kitchen, a room away from the piano.

"This morning I awoke and opened the crystal on my watch to feel what time it was," Bert continued. "One hand was straight up and the other was straight down, so I thought it was six o'clock, time to get up. I felt for my stick next to the bed where I always keep it, and I got out of bed." In his perpetual darkness he had adeptly stepped toward the bathroom, showered, and dressed in clean pants and a clean shirt. He then counted each stair as he climbed them to the kitchen. Before starting to make his own breakfast, he thought to check his watch again.

"It was then that I realized I'd read my watch wrong. It wasn't time for breakfast at all. It was the middle of the night. So then I had to go back to bed." He laughed now, at his mistake. "I didn't get much sleep."

Bert was still cheerful in spite of being tired. He didn't complain about his quandaries, he merely described them as they were. He talked about others, too, some from the past. "I used to go to the movies, years ago," he said. "I really couldn't enjoy them like everybody else. At parties I was scared to move around for fear that I would bump into things and knock them over. I would just stand in one place. Then people would seat me way across the room from where the action was. They didn't understand that I was lost from what was going on.

"By the time I came to Colorado, I was run-down from taking care of Helen and from forty years of pretending to be like everybody else when I couldn't hear or see. Now with interpreters like you, I'm getting what I never had before. When you sign to me, I can hear the words in my head like you are talking to me."

"I *am* talking to you," I signed in his hands.

"Yes, you are talking to me."

"You-me-need-work-now."

"Yes, I'll shut up now," he laughed.

As the teacher, I was always trying to get Bert back on track for our sign language lessons. However, he was always teaching me lessons too—about life. Before we ended our session, Bert reminded me how our human behavior can be harmful or helpful to ourselves.

"You can initiate a state of great happiness by compelling it," he said, as he lifted his hands high. "You can raise your arms into the air like this, and you can say, '*I feel great!*'" He told me how, years ago, he sat next to the radio mesmerized, listening to Timothy Stone, a prominent businessman in Chicago. "When he talked, people listened," Bert said. "He motivated wayward kids through speeches at the boys' clubs. When I heard him say this on the radio, I stood in my living room and raised my hands up, too."

As we ended our lesson on that note, I drove away wanting to lift my arms into the air and shout out, too, but it was Bert's other words that were singing in my heart. *When you sign to me, I can hear the words in my head.* After more than a year of sign language lessons, we had broken through his sound barrier.

Language

They [books] tell me so much that is interesting about things I cannot see, and they are never tired or troubled like people.
—HELEN KELLER, *The Story of My Life*

While reading Helen Keller's autobiography, *The Story of My Life,* I brought up the book as a topic for discussion with Bert. He said he didn't know much about Helen Keller, other than she was blind and deaf. I thought Bert might be interested in the letters Anne Sullivan, Helen's teacher, wrote to Sophia C. Hopkins at the Perkins Institute for the Blind about her early lessons with young Helen.

Anne described Helen as quick-tempered and willful. Frustrated from inadequate means of communication, Helen behaved like "a little savage" who had "tyrannized over everybody." Yet it was clear from the start that Helen was a bright child. After Helen discovered a doll in her teacher's trunk, Anne spelled d-o-l-l into Helen's hand. Without understanding what the spelling meant, Helen copied back the finger movements immediately. What followed was an awakening of a human being. When given language, Helen transformed from a "wild little creature" into a beguiling child, and then into an educated adult, who later became an author, spokeswoman, and ambassador for social issues throughout the world.

I hoped that Anne Sullivan's letters depicting Helen's extraordinary language development might impress upon Bert how difficult it is to acquire language when you can't hear it. I hoped he'd appreciate the feat Helen Keller accomplished and would see that he had accomplished feats of his own.

I was disheartened to learn that the braille library didn't have *The Story of My Life*. Braille books are expensive to publish and, with little demand, the selection is extremely limited. But how, then, was I to share this story with Bert? I'd have to pick out my favorite parts of Anne Sullivan's letters and either convey them in sign language or use the machine to braille them myself.

I brought the book with me to the next session with Bert. After a couple of failed attempts in using sign to capture the spirit of her letters, I reluctantly gave in to the braille machine. Some parts deserved a word-for-word translation, and sign language with Bert was too slow. I began describing Anne's first meeting with the deaf-blind six-year-old—the day Helen met Annie on the porch and took her bag, searching for candy. I described the infamous scene at the dining room table where Helen walked from person to person, grabbing whatever she wanted from their plates. I related how Annie trained Helen to use a spoon. After dragging her over to retrieve the spoon from wherever Helen kept flinging the utensil, Annie physically restrained Helen in the chair, insisting she use the spoon to feed herself. By the time Annie got Helen to fold her napkin and eat like a lady at the table, the room was a shamble from all of their tussling. Anne was exhausted.

I paraphrased from the book, typing words into the brailler as fast as Bert could read them with his finger. After interpreting all day with other clients and twenty or thirty minutes of brailing, my neck and shoulder muscles were aching but I wanted to keep going. Bert, however, paused from the brailler. He leaned back in the chair and shook his head in astonishment. He hadn't seen Patty Duke's portrayal of Helen and Anne Bancroft's performance as Anne Sullivan in Arthur Penn's 1962 film *The Miracle Worker*. He contemplated the story for a minute. "Are you exhausted when you work with me?" he asked with a worried laugh.

"You give me e-n-e-r—," I spelled.

He finished the word for me. "Energy," he said, relieved.

I smiled, patting him. I set his hand back onto the brailler and continued typing. "Annie began spending all her moments with Helen, spelling into her hand, trying to tame the child who had tyrannized everyone in her midst. Anne spelled to her just as naturally and often as a mother talked to her infant until she grasped the understanding of language and began to use it on her own."

Bert wanted to know how Annie did the spelling. I showed him her method of communication, which was solely fingerspelling by forming the letters quickly one after the other. It was too fast for Bert to read. He thought deeply about the method, visualizing Annie spelling words and associating them with objects until Helen finally grasped their meaning. At that moment, Bert shifted his profound reverence for poet Robert Smithdas, who had already obtained language before becoming deaf, to Helen Keller, who had virtually no language input until the age of six. For the next two lessons, we read Anne Sullivan's letters.

It amazed Bert to learn that after three months, Helen's vocabulary grew to four hundred words. After one year, it expanded to nine hundred words. Bert had acquired fewer than three hundred signed words after one year. I explained that Helen had an advantage over other deaf children because she always had Annie at her side, feeding her language.

Bert and I saw that the more language Helen acquired, the deeper she reflected. She began to ask questions, hundreds of them. She wanted to know about the sky and about day and night, about the ocean and the mountains. She became interested in colors. When Annie told Helen that her little sister had blue eyes, Helen asked, "Are they like wee skies?"

At this Bert fell silent. He shook his head and his eyes filled with tears. "That's the most beautiful thing I've ever heard," he cried.

The impact of what Bert and I managed to accomplish in eighteen months and how Helen and Anne had triumphed hit us both. Tears streamed down my face. I lifted Bert's hands to the wetness on my cheek and the hushed sobs of my shoulders. For the first time, Bert was without words.

Diagnosis: Breast Cancer

When there were two weeks left in September, I got the idea to document Bert's activities on video. The warm weather would be coming to an end soon and with the trees in a vibrant array of fall colors, it would be a great time to film outdoor vignettes of Bert with his friends. John and Mary were agreeable to my idea. However, the week I had planned to start the project, my calendar suddenly filled up. It was our son's last season of high school soccer, and Jim and I became all consumed with his activities.

Matthew had aspirations of playing soccer for a Division 1 school out of state. He dreamed of a scholarship, and this was the critical time to be filling out applications and visiting schools. Frantically, we arranged last-minute trips. Over one weekend Matthew and I flew into Boston and traveled to the University of Massachusetts at Amherst, the University of New Hampshire, and to the University of Rhode Island. A couple of weeks later, Jim and Matt flew to Bradley University, in Illinois. After their return, we were into the third game of Matt's season when he suffered an injury to his leg.

As Matt hobbled into the doctor's office on crutches, we carried the sinking feeling of a ruined dream. Until an MRI pinpointed the extent of the injury, we wrestled with the possibility that all of our efforts devoted to soccer for the past seven years were for naught. Matt's injury turned out to be a twisted and bruised knee, which required only a couple weeks of rest to heal. But because Matt was the integral force on the midfield, his team missed him sorely. Jim and I were relieved that the injury wasn't more serious, yet we'd been thrown for a loop.

Bert kindly listened to me carry on about my son and he offered me encouragement. "He'll do well," he said. "He has a good family and his parents are setting good examples." His faith and reassurance were heartening.

Bert often helped me in that way. Sometimes I arrived all frazzled from driving in the city, fitting in construction errands between interpreting assignments and soccer games. I felt like I was going in six different directions. My body raced to keep up with my mind that was going a hundred miles per hour. An environment that overstimulated me didn't faze Bert in the least. In his very different world, he didn't see masses of people hurrying around and cars going at a clip in all directions. There were no billboards competing for his attention over car radios, or music blaring from cars stuck in traffic. He didn't see the television or front-page headlines sensationalizing the latest story. He didn't fall victim to the glitz and glamour on the magazine covers at the grocery checkout. Bert did not have to contend with the rat race of society, and when I was with him he brought me into his serene world.

After fifteen minutes with Bert, my heart rate returned to a healthy level. Pressures disappeared, replaced with laughter and love. A visit with Bert was like an elixir that helped me take a breath, slow down, and appreciate the small things in life. I always left him feeling better than when I arrived.

The busy weeks of fall pressed on. In spite of Bert's calming effect on me, I came down with a nasty cold and had to miss a lesson. Shortly after, I missed another lesson when I was struck with a migraine that kept me in bed all day. It wasn't typical for me to be sick, and I had never missed a session with Bert. I hated canceling lessons because I believed Bert deserved every possible minute of communication. He had so much of life to catch up on— there were no moments to throw away. Luckily, I was soon back to work, making up for the time we'd lost.

At the end of soccer season I was enjoying the reprieve before the holiday season when I got a call from the radiologist at the women's clinic. I'd had a routine mammogram there ten days earlier.

"We found some microcalcifications on the X-ray," she said, in a kind, professional tone. "It could mean there's something going on there."

For a few seconds I didn't have any idea what she was talking about. After I'd had the mammogram, I'd put it completely out of my mind. I didn't know who she was nor did I know what microcalcifications were. But she was entreating me to come in for a biopsy.

The radiologist said it looked like calcium on my X-ray and she needed to take a better look at it. I thought she was overreacting—calling me about "calcium." At first I was reluctant, but finally I agreed to go in for the biopsy. In the meantime, however, I wanted to find out what this might mean. I went to the library. Nervously I checked out several books on breast cancer and read them in the days before my appointment. I thought the knowledge would make me more at ease with having the biopsy, but it didn't. I learned too much. I learned what microcalcifications were.

The radiologist's suspicions were correct. After the biopsy, she called with the results. "It's DCIS," she said. "Ductal carcinoma in situ."

I was silent. I'd just learned what ductal carcinoma in situ was, and I knew that carcinoma was another word for cancer. I felt my face grow hot and my heart start pounding. I wrote down everything she said because I knew I wouldn't remember our conversation after I hung up.

She continued. "The good news is, the cancer is still in the ducts—it hasn't spread." The bad news was, it was aggressive. She also said I would need surgery.

I was forty-six years old—too young to get breast cancer, I thought. Why me? How could this happen? How would this affect my kids and how would I tell Bert? What would he do without me? I needed to see him every week. We had too much to do.

I kept the awful secret about my cancer between Jim and myself for almost two weeks, until I realized that my denying it was not going to make it go away. As the doctor's words, *carcinoma, aggressive, multifocal,* rang over in my mind, I knew I was going to have to divulge to people that I had this terrible thing.

After a long sleepless night, I arrived a half hour early for my morning session with Bert. The door was unlocked, so I let myself in. "Hello," I called, expecting to hear from Mary upstairs. It was only eight-thirty, but she was already gone. As I headed down the stairs my heart raced with scattered anxiety. Bert wasn't at our table near the end of the staircase where he usually waited for me, so I scurried past and hastened to John's adjoining office.

The door was open and I found John busy at the computer. I didn't wait for an invitation to enter and even sidestepped our normal, cheerful "Good morning." I dropped onto the first available chair. Giving him no chance to react to my dramatic entrance, I blurted out, short of breath,

"John, I have to talk to you. I have bad news." I didn't even offer an apology for interrupting his work. Unfazed by the disruption, he continued what he was doing for a minute before turning around to acknowledge me. Before he could say anything at all, my harbored anxiety spilled out in a burst of emotion. "I have breast cancer!"

John's jaw dropped and his body froze. He didn't utter a word, so I kept on talking. "The doctor is telling me that they caught it early and that's good, but I have to have surgery. I don't know when. I should be okay after the surgery," I added, trying to lessen the shock. "There's still another spot she's concerned about, but she doesn't know if it's the same thing. I have to have another biopsy—"

John finally caught his breath. "Diane, I've just been researching breast cancer for my latest consulting project," he said, rolling his chair toward me. "They've made some great strides in treatment. It's good that they found yours early! That's a very good thing."

I tried to explain the sketchy details of what I understood about my condition. "I'm so scared," I finally admitted, breaking down into the tears that had been unshed since receiving my diagnosis. "I haven't told my kids. This is an important time for Matthew, his senior year. I can't tell him."

"Why can't you tell him?"

"He has too much pressure on him. He has SAT tests . . . a tournament in San Diego. He's trying to pick a college."

"What would happen if you told him?"

"I guess . . . he would handle it . . . but how are we going to tell Bert?" My arms and hands were useless as I tried using them to mop up the flood that was streaming from my eyes and nose. John scrambled around the room for some tissues.

"I didn't sleep all night. I was so afraid," I cried, wiping my eyes as the tears kept coming. He handed me another tissue and reached out to give me a hug.

"What are you afraid of?" he asked.

I blubbered something into his shoulder about a grotesque image of the cancer eating me alive. "I don't want my family to have to watch me die from this."

John held onto me. The bulk of his shoulder and his gentle strength gave me the calmness I needed that morning. While John and I had been talking, Bert had positioned himself at our work table. He sat patiently waiting for me, oblivious to the fact that I had arrived.

John and I agreed that we would tell Bert about my situation later, after we knew more. There were still too many unknowns and no reason to burden Bert with this information now. I drew in a deep breath, left John in his office, and went out to greet Bert.

We had our lesson as usual that morning while, in the back of my mind, I was thinking about what John had said. I knew he was right. I didn't need to protect Matthew; I had to tell him. I decided that Jim and I would inform both our kids at the same time. It would have to be on Sunday when Heather would be home from college.

• • • • •

We informed the kids at the dinner table. I told them the doctor had found something on my mammogram and that I would most likely be having surgery soon. At first they were quiet but then Heather asked, "Is it breast cancer?" She broke out crying immediately when I said *yes,* but Matt stared straight ahead at the television. He came to me later that evening to talk privately, after he'd had time to process what I'd said. After breaking the news to the kids, I'd gotten over the first couple of hurdles, but there would be more. I would have to tell Bert, too.

But I couldn't tell him. It was too hard. Instead, we continued our lessons as usual while I underwent the second biopsy on the other suspicious area. I didn't want to tell Bert my life had taken this sudden detour, because being with him felt like the only thing normal on this path. In between a multitude of medical appointments, I was voraciously reading a stack of books in an effort to educate myself about breast cancer. I had decisions to make.

After the second biopsy substantiated additional DCIS, with cancer in two places in one breast, a lumpectomy would not be safe. I prepared for an inevitable mastectomy and I would choose reconstructive surgery.

Perfect Ending or Perfect Beginning?

As Thanksgiving neared, I wrestled with how to break the news to my brothers and sisters. I dreaded having to deal with their individual reactions. Before I could tell them, my younger brother, Scott, called with more disturbing news. He was at the emergency room with my father.

"Dad has fluid on his lungs," Scott said. "He was having trouble breathing and we barely made it here in time!"

I pictured what was to come. Dad had always made it clear that he was wholly satisfied with the life he'd lived and wasn't interested in any heroics to save it when his time came. For most of his life he had avoided medical intervention and was at peace with that decision. Now, faced with an awful sense of suffocating, Dad willingly allowed the doctors in the emergency room to medicate him, easing his labored breathing. In his weakened state, he reluctantly agreed to be admitted into the hospital.

Heather and I made the fifty-minute trip to Denver to see him the next day. Scott and my sister Margie met us at the hospital where we found Dad in an irritable mood, fidgeting and fussing at the nurses about the oxygen tube and the numerous wires attached to him. These were especially unnerving to Dad, a man with obsessive-compulsive tendencies. I was surprised by how pale and exhausted he looked. Although a smoker, he always kept himself in meticulous physical condition by walking, playing golf, and gardening.

The doctors ordered several tests, including an ultrasound. In spite of Dad's impatience and anxiety, he managed to cooperate. Margie and I peeked in at Dad from the doorway. He lay calmly, watching his heart beating on the monitor, seemingly intrigued by the technology. I trembled with tension.

After all the tests, the doctors told Dad he needed a valve replacement in his heart. They would use a valve from a pig, and the surgery would give him five to ten more years. Without it, he might live only days, and at most a few months. But Dad wasn't interested in the surgery. He asked Scott to take him home.

That night with Jim, I sorted through the events of recent weeks. In the privacy of our bedroom I became overwhelmed by their magnitude. How could I ever find enough strength to deal with my father's imminent passing and get through my own crisis at the same time?

"My *Dad* is going to die," I cried. When my knees buckled under, Jim caught me before I fell to the floor, sobbing. His body, strong from years of construction work, easily handled my dead weight. He had to hold me up. I was doubled over, wracked with grief. "I can't do both of these," I gasped.

Growing up I'd been afraid of my dad because he had a drinking problem. Our childhood was tough. Dad was strict and our family had little money. He didn't do many activities with us, but the things he did do were special, like when he went swimming with us or started water fights in the backyard. When I was sick with measles, tonsillitis, strep throat, earaches, or migraines, he brought me cold drinks. In my teen years he quit drinking, but by then I often found him annoying, stubborn, and even embarrassing.

Dad had an incredible baritone singing voice. He sang when he was shaving. I'd hear him sing, "Smile for Me, My Diane." He had a fun sense of humor and a sweet side, too. After I was married and had my own family, when I stopped by his house with the kids or by myself, whether he was mowing the lawn, pruning bushes, raking leaves, or cooking, he was always happy to see me. We'd often sit in his living room and have long talks, where mostly I'd listen to his opinions or hear him reminisce. Afterward he'd find something for me to take home—freshly cut roses, plants, or a sack of potatoes (he'd buy one and get the second one free).

Some people thought my dad was difficult, for he was opinionated and blunt. Some thought him odd because he retired from law at age forty-five, disillusioned with the profession. He spoke with distain for "the bureaucrats in the government" and with open distrust of medical professionals.

In spite of all his peculiarities, I understood and loved my dad. He had high morals and integrity, and I respected him. I was not ready to let go of him. As I cried in Jim's arms, he comforted me the best way he knew how. "This is your Dad's decision," he said, referring to Dad's not wanting surgery. "He's always made his wishes known. This is how he wants it."

I knew he was right. Jim's steadfast reassurance and the care and understanding from John and Mary sustained me through the next few weeks while I waited for my surgery. In my anxiety, it felt like a year.

I continued to struggle with when to tell Bert that I had breast cancer, and I hid my sadness from him about my father's condition. I wanted to protect Bert from the anxiety and pain. Subconsciously, I was protecting myself. If you don't talk about your problems, you can pretend they're not there. Had I not learned anything from Bert about pretending?

John and Mary respected my wishes and said they would follow my lead about when to tell Bert. In the meantime, I continued to avoid telling him. Our lessons were a reprieve from all the worry. I could focus on what I loved doing, and I was always happy when I was with Bert. At the end of each day, when I could no longer hold myself together, Jim was there to pick me up.

Right before Thanksgiving, I told my brothers and sisters about my situation. Luckily, there wasn't the hysteria I'd imagined. Thanksgiving, however, was celebrated with a pall over it, like we were just going through the motions. We ate at Jim's sister's house in Denver, without Dad. "I don't want to be the center of attention," he had said. After dinner, we took him some leftovers before heading back to the mountains.

• • • • •

I counted the days to my operation, to put the bad dream behind me. Finally it came. The forty-eight hours after surgery were all a blur until the phone rang. Through the fog in my head I heard a faraway voice on the line.

"Diane, it's Mary," she said. "Bert wants to talk to you." They had told Bert about me. I lay in my hospital bed, waiting with the phone to my ear while she put him on.

"Diane … John told me about you. How are you?" His voice was sad. "I need you. I need you to get well soon and come back to our lessons. I miss you. I hope you are doing okay. I love you."

I knew Bert couldn't hear me on the phone, promising to be back soon, but I said it anyway.

Jim brought me home four days after the surgery. There were bouquets of flowers everywhere, cards and letters waiting for me. Lying on the couch I read them one by one, including Bert's.

Dear Diane,

One does not truly appreciate the value of a great friend until there is an interruption in that relationship. You have been such an integral part of my life since I came to Colorado that I find it hard not to see you as usual. I hope that by this time you are home, in the loving hands of your great family. I never forget the early days of our sign sessions. You helped breathe life back into me. Nobody has ever done so much for me at that particular phase of my difficult recovery. You were always so cheerful and wise, that I really felt blessed. Now, I am hoping that your recovery is fast and we can get back to that wonderful relationship. I realize the problems you may have had throughout this period and naturally felt pained for you.

What a tremendous storm we have had. It reminds me of the time you told me the story about Jim, walking a mile through four feet of snow to get home because his truck was stuck. I shall never forget this sample of nature today. There is great beauty to it all and this land of ours needs this liquid for a good life. Take care of yourself Diane, and I hope that soon I will be seeing you. Love, Bert.

Beginning my recovery, I realized how unprepared I was for the physical debilitation that followed. The vitality I had so much taken for granted had been sucked away by the surgery. Walking across a room left me winded. Sitting at the table for a meal made my heart race like I'd just run a mile. Our sliding glass doors were too heavy for me to let the dogs outside, and I couldn't even pull the blankets up from the bottom of the bed to cover myself. There was no energy to parent my teenage son. When he asked a question or pleaded to borrow the car, I couldn't even think to make decisions.

I had lost control over my life and was angry at the world. I worried about my lack of strength and mobility. I didn't believe I would ever feel normal again. Sitting on a stool in the shower, too frail to stand, I wept, wondering what had happened to me. I let myself emote while the tears washed away in the warm water. After a few minutes Bert came to my mind. I had never seen him cry about having Usher Syndrome. Suddenly my losing a breast seemed like nothing compared to Bert's losing his sight and his hearing. I pulled myself together. I would get through this.

I'd been home from the hospital for a week but was still too fragile to attend Bert's eighty-eighth birthday party on December 12. Instead I sent a fax for John and Mary to translate into braille:

Dear Bert,
Today is your birthday and I wanted to be there to celebrate it with you. I am very excited that you are having your 88th birthday. You and I have very much to celebrate. Yes, I know that I helped breathe life back into you, and I watched you blossom. Although you already had it in

you, you were just looking for the way. You found the way. I've watched you for a year and a half and you uplift me every time I see you. Now I'm very weak, I have been through a traumatic experience. John and Mary have been my cheerleaders and I'm using you as my role model to help me rebound.

The positive energy from my family and my friends is getting me through this and I'm finding a little more strength every day. I feel my recuperation is going painfully slow, but Jim tells me that I'm improving daily. I don't know when we can resume our lessons, but I look forward to our first visit. I hope you have a very Happy Birthday. Please eat a piece of cake for me. Love, Diane.

John and Mary waited for two and a half weeks before asking if they could bring Bert to visit me. Even though I was still having trouble moving around and felt too weak to entertain visitors, I couldn't say no. I napped for three hours before their visit. Heather arrived from college just as I was getting myself up and trying to comb the tangles from my overgrown hair. She'd driven six hours to be home for Christmas.

I inundated her with tears, so happy to finally have her home. We were still holding onto each other when I mentioned that John and Mary were bringing Bert over. "I need you to help me vacuum and put out some snacks," I said.

Matthew came home, too, and then the Riedels showed up at the door with Christmas gifts and a poinsettia. They had brought Andrea along, and she helped Bert up the step to the doorway. This was his first visit to our house.

"Don't sign, don't sign," he said, in his merry way. He didn't want me to hurt my sore back and pectoral muscles. I managed a smile as he gave me a gentle hug.

I led Bert to a chair in the dining room. Surprisingly, signing was not painful or difficult, and much to my relief, the anesthesia hadn't wiped out all my memory of sign language. The visit from my good friends was wholly therapeutic, and we were all in a festive mood when Jim came home from work. He was surprised to see us having a party with Christmas music playing in the background.

The music came from a CD of Bert playing a selection of his favorite Christmas carols. While I was in the hospital, the Riedels had been over to Rich and Andrea's house for dinner. Andrea offered Bert a scotch and then invited him to try out their piano. As snowflakes fell, Bert began a medley of carols inside their cozy home. Andrea and Mary sang along to "Oh Come, All Ye Faithful" from the kitchen as they finished preparing the meal. One song was enough for Rich, the accomplished musician, to recognize an opportunity. Spontaneously, he took advantage of Bert's impromptu Christmas concert and began recording what became Bert's first CD. Singing and laughing filled the rest of their evening, which grew into a gift for all of Bert's friends—a timeless reminder of him that we shall cherish forever. To our house they brought their music, friendship, and love. Jim smiled when he recognized Bert on the cover of the CD wearing a Santa Claus hat.

• • • • •

On Christmas Day I finally saw my dad. The family didn't come to our house as usual. We celebrated at Jim's mother's house in Denver—we were too concerned about Dad's heart and what effect the high altitude of Conifer might have on him. All of us were aware that this was likely to be the last family gathering with my father. Dad and I hugged, apologizing for not visiting each other—neither of us had had the emotional or physical strength to be very supportive to one another. Even now we were both a little reserved. We didn't know what else to say. Nevertheless, I was happy to be there for this special time.

A few days later I felt a bit of my old self returning. By New Year's Day I was ready to resume teaching. My mobility was still limited for driving, so Andrea brought Bert to my house that evening. Because he was rarely invited out, or to anyone's home, it was a special occasion for Bert. He was more animated and cheery than ever and right away made friends with my two dogs, who discovered that Bert kept doggie treats in his pocket. After he'd given each of them one, Keisha, my husky, kept jumping on his lap for more. Laughing at her spunk, Bert gave her two more treats and then held out a third. "Give this one to the little dog," he said. I got a good laugh out of that. My other dog, Thule, was a big overweight lab. Because she didn't jump on him with the same vigor as Keisha, he pictured her as "little."

At the table I tried to concentrate on our sign language lesson, but Bert was having too much fun. He decided he wanted to dance. "Dance?" I signed.

"Yes, to celebrate the New Year."

So we did. We danced in my living room next to the sparkling colored lights on our Christmas tree while Bert sang "Auld Lang Syne."

"I wish you could see my tree," I signed.

"Is it big?"

"Yes." With his hand on mine, I pointed to the sky, knowing Bert had no way to judge how tall it was. "My tree goes up to the ceiling." With my palms, I demonstrated our cathedral ceiling—my fingertips touching at its peak.

"How tall is it?" he asked.

"Fourteen feet. The lights are blinking." I thought dancing with Bert was the perfect ending to the year, or perhaps the perfect beginning to a new one.

Angels

My father passed away on January 6. He was seventy-six. I couldn't help but reflect on the differences between Bert and my dad. Dad was totally at peace with his decision to let nature run its course, and he was looking forward to being in heaven with my mother. At eighty-eight Bert still exuded energy and a zest for life. "I want to live! I have goals I want to accomplish," he often said. I respected both Dad's and Bert's perspectives. One was not better or worse than the other.

My dad accomplished his last goal, in September, four months before he died. That goal was placing my mother's ashes in a resting spot. It had been four years since Mom passed away and three years since we got her ashes back from the anatomical society, to whom she donated her body. Dad wanted to scatter her ashes then, in his rose garden next to the house. He lovingly attended to those roses. But my siblings didn't want them there. None of us could agree on that particular spot, or any other, for Mom's ashes. My sister Margie didn't want them in the garden because "Mom never liked that house," she said. So Dad just left the box with her ashes in a back bedroom of the house, where they sat for three years.

Then one day, Father Jim from Mom's church appeared at my dad's doorstep. Father Jim didn't even have to say what he came for. Dad told him, "Whatever you need, you've got it." Dad hadn't attended church in years but had respected Mom's dedication to hers and was prepared for whatever the minister might want. It was money. Father Jim wanted to renovate part of the church building for a preschool and build an adjoining playground. Later that day, Dad, all my siblings, and I made a unanimous decision to build the playground in honor of Mom, and that's where we would place her ashes.

The sun shone in the blue September sky on the day of this private dedication. The leaves were just beginning to change color and they sparkled in the light breeze. Nothing felt more perfect. That morning we had placed a white pedestal with a cherub statue in the corner of the playground. Now the cherub stood as guardian of the children who would play there.

While Matthew sat on the end of the children's slide and Jim leaned against the kids' climbing structure, the rest of the family gathered around. Each of my siblings, including myself, spoke.

"What is so fitting about the cherub and this setting," I said, reminding my brothers and sisters, "is that Mom used to work here when the church preschool was the Denver School for the Vision and Hearing Handicapped program. Although Mom was the secretary for the school, she was like an angel who spent a lot of time with the children and loved every one of them: three-year-old Morgan, born without eyeballs; Miranda, with cerebral palsy, born blind and deaf; and each of the others."

During the three years she worked at the school, Mom and the other teachers often took the children to the pool. I accompanied them a few times when I was just learning sign language. Swimming with Mom and the little blind and deaf-blind kids was one of the things that inspired me to go into my interpreting career.

Referring to Mom as an angel must have resonated with Dad because at the end of the dedication he said with an emotional sparkle in his eye, "I've never been a religious man, but I've started to watch *Touched by an Angel.* My wife gave me these fine children and now with this playground she has breathed new life back into this church. I am the happiest man on earth." It was a spiritual transformation for Dad. Closing this chapter in his life, he was ready to join my mother. We didn't know it would be just four months away.

Two days after my father died, we held his memorial service. My heart leaped when I saw John leading Bert into the church among the crowd of people. I was surprised and touched that they had come because the Riedels never met Dad.

Father Jim began the service with a homily about my dad and his involvement with the new preschool. Chris spoke, too, giving an emotional tribute to my father.

While I listened from the front row with my family, I was cognizant that John and Bert were near the back of the church—sitting without an interpreter. I wanted so badly to be next to Bert, signing everything my brother was saying to the congregation. But Bert had no experience with professional interpreting. Interpretation of a memorial service flows rapidly. Jean and I worked with Bert in a different capacity. We taught and conversed with him slowly, using sign language. It's totally different from interpreting. I contented myself knowing John would sign a little during the service and Bert would be patient. John and I would tell Bert about the service later.

Wearing a double-breasted blue suit with gold buttons, my brother spoke from the pulpit summarizing eloquently just who my father was, including his flaws along with his positive attributes. "He was a butcher, a grocer, and a lawyer. He served his country as a lieutenant in the anti-tank company in World War II and returned with honor. He was an avid golfer, a pathetic fisherman, a dedicated gardener, and a 'gourmet' chef."

Some of us laughed because we knew Dad wasn't really a gourmet chef. He was just fastidious. After we moved Mom to a nursing home and he was cooking for himself, he would line up his fish sticks perfectly in a baking dish, with the exact same number each time. He'd slice an apple just so and place the sections in a precise pattern atop a bowl of cottage cheese. And the "Bernie burgers" he cooked for Scott and his partner, Peter, were served every Saturday night at 6:30 without fail.

"Bernie Schilt never met a stranger," Chris said, meaning he talked to anyone (except salesmen), "and he was always free with advice. His advice was always sound and right on. And if we had followed his advice, which most of us did not, we would have been better off every time. He never wavered in his beliefs. He instilled in us the value of money, independence, and confidence. Dad knew it all, and if you were a great listener, you were communicating with Dad. Unfortunately, he never got to know the real us. Yet he loved us and we loved him. He made it hard to love him, but we did. . . ."

Chris described how Dad, as he had in life, choreographed his death. "Per his wishes, we had Dad moved to a hospice toward the very end. Falling in and out of consciousness, he smiled when Margie told him where he was. We prayed for a swift and peaceful ending, and our prayers were answered."

At the end of Dad's service, Margie invited the congregation to reconvene outside on the playground. She

Bert and I talking at my father's funeral.

explained that the playground was dedicated to Mom and that Dad's ashes would be placed there, too. More than a hundred of us crowded the small play area. My sister Jeanie spotted John in the assembly and called out to me, "Diane, John is over there with Bert."

With a burst of adrenaline, I found my way over to the door where they had come out of the preschool. I took Bert's hand. A big smile emerged on his face when he recognized me. After almost two hours of Bert sitting on a dark quiet bench inside the church, his quiet was broken. I signed into his hand. "I want show you a-n-g-e-l, s-t-a-t-u-e for my mother." I led him up the steps to the playground. Everyone's eyes were on us. My Dad's neighbor took our picture. "We are on p-l-a-y g-r-o-u-n-d next to small g-a-r-d-e-n. This is a-n-g-e-l." I placed his hands on the cherub statue. My two sisters came running over to meet Bert. They'd heard so much about him.

"My sisters and brothers want to meet you," I signed. I called my brothers over. One by one, Bert and John met Margie, Jeanie, Chris, and Scott. It surprised me when Jeanie said, "I love you, Bert."

It was two more weeks before we got a printed copy of my brother's eulogy transposed into braille for Bert. During my first lesson back after my surgery and Dad's death, I could tell Bert was troubled by the tone of the eulogy. He couldn't understand why my father had quit working at such a young age and made it so hard for people to love him. I have a difficult enough time describing who my father was to sighted and hearing people. I felt it practically impossible to convey this to Bert. It wasn't something I could handle right then, so I changed the subject.

Many times I compared Bert and my father. They were of the same generation. Both were involved in the stock market. Both were committed to their families. Both were intelligent men with integrity. I often wished for them to meet. Bert wanted to meet my dad. And while Dad often asked me about Bert, he never requested to meet him. I knew he didn't have the patience or interest to learn to communicate on a braille machine. Unlike Bert, he had no desire to try new things. I had to accept that my wish for them to meet would never come true.

Suspended in Space

Blindness cuts people off from things;
deafness cuts people off from people.

—HELEN KELLER

The words I'd been waiting to hear came from the oncologist at the end of January. Three months had passed since my diagnosis. "You don't need chemotherapy," he said, "and there's no indication that tamoxifen will benefit you either." The hour consultation was all I needed to put the whole ordeal behind me. I thanked him and was out of there. I had dwelled on my cancer long enough and was ready to get back to normal.

Returning to a regular schedule at the Riedels' felt great. I'd been away since Thanksgiving and it seemed like a homecoming to work with John and Mary once more on their sign language. Bert was happy about it, too. "It's good to have you back," he said during those early weeks. "I feel on a wavelength with you. I feel safe, not suspended in space."

For the first time, Bert shared his thoughts on his own hospitalization when he broke his neck and went into rehabilitation at the Life Care Center. "People brought me food and that was nice. And they talked to me on the machine and that was nice." But as strangers, he said, they were merely "dots on a page."

"Others were too afraid to even try typing on the machine," Bert continued. "One person came in to talk to me, and she couldn't type. She indicated that she knew sign language by moving her hands in mine, but I couldn't understand her. I tried to guess some things that she might've been asking. I went through the letters of the alphabet and told her to stop me when I came to the letter she wanted. I tried to figure out ways we could communicate. Then I thought she would just leave. Instead, she stayed a long time. It felt miserable."

It had been more than a year since Bert experienced those not-so-pleasant times at the Life Care Center; it hadn't dawned on him then that without physical contact, he couldn't perceive a person's affect or body language through a braille machine alone—the things that make people interesting, unique, and human. Now, however, I saw how far he had come with sign language in the twenty-two months I'd known him, and in his understanding of the communication barrier that had plagued him nearly all his life. I decided to explore this more deeply by bringing his attention to a quote by Helen Keller. "What do you think about this q-u-o-t-e," I asked.

"What quote is that?"

"Blindness cuts people off from— "

"Oh that's very negative. I wouldn't pay any attention to that quote," he said.

"No, Bert," I said aloud, and started again, spelling in his hand, "H-e-l-e-n- K-e-l-l-e-r said that."

"I'm sure Helen Keller would never say something like that."

"There is more. I was not finished," I signed.

Bert shifted his attention to a different quote. "I don't know who said this quote: 'God give me the wisdom to accept the things I cannot change—'"

"That is not q-u-o-t-e I talk about. I try tell you about different q-u-o-t-e; H-e-l-e-n- K-e-l-l-e-r."

"What quote are you talking about?" he asked.

This time he let me finish. "Blindness cuts people off from things, but deafness cuts people off from people."

"Ohhh . . ." His expression got serious while he thought about it. "People can live without sight," he said. "When I lost my sight, I listened to *The Rise and the Fall of the Roman Empire* on the recorder. I loved it. I had talking books, I had friends, and I had my music. Blind people can potentiate their hearing and their smell. They can recognize people by their walk or by their scent or their voice, and they can excel intellectually. I think sound is the most beautiful sense in our body.

"Hearing stimulates the brain," he went on. "It allows us to process and evaluate, to become scholarly. That's why Robert Smithdas and Helen Keller are so remarkable. They did it without hearing. For me, sound is preferable to sight for joy in my life. I miss hearing a child's voice. I miss hearing my music and I miss conversation. And now without my hearing or my sight, I miss the life I was once a part of. But when you give the gift of sign language to a deaf-blind old man, that's life! It's like a mother giving birth to a child. I was scared of sign language in the beginning. Now I look forward to our sign talk. When understanding flows, you have real life."

Helen Keller became deaf and blind as a toddler, after an illness. Perhaps she was too young to have been able to remember sounds like Bert.

Bert missed hearing children's voices, and he missed music. But was his hearing loss ever life threatening? When one of my deaf friends lost his keys because he didn't hear them drop, it wasn't life threatening, it was an annoyance.

When he drove his hearing daughters to school while the car horn was stuck blaring, and they didn't think to tell him because they trusted he knew what he was doing, that was an embarrassment. When a deaf woman in a hotel room didn't hear the water running from the faucet all night, stepped out of bed in the morning into three inches of soaked carpet, was that an annoyance, an embarrassment, or a hazard?

When does deafness become life threatening? Was it life threatening for the deaf-blind woman who signed to the doctor, while I spoke her words, asking what she could do about preventing the disease that causes women to hunch over? She signed it by pointing her index finger up, then slowing bending it over.

"Take calcium. You can buy it over the counter," the doctor responded hurriedly, before he left the examination room. I signed his words into her hands, wondering which calcium he meant—oyster shell or bone meal? Chelated or citrate? With magnesium or without? How many milligrams? Weren't some more easily absorbed than others?

"What's calcium?" she signed.

"The doctor is gone now," I said. It wasn't in my professional role to describe all the different kinds of calcium and suggest which one might be best for her.

Another time, I was interpreting for a deaf woman who was seeing her doctor for a yearly physical, when the doctor asked her if she was interested in hormone replacement therapy.

"What's that?" the woman asked.

The doctor paused for a moment. I started preparing to interpret what I envisioned would be a long explanation on the role of estrogen in the female reproductive system, the symptoms of its gradual decline, the increased risks of cardiovascular disease and osteoporosis in post-menopausal women, and the benefits of replacement hormones combined with various treatment approaches and their side effects. Last, I thought he might explain the controversy over whether their use creates an increased risk of endometrial and breast cancers. Instead, the doctor said, "Wait a minute," and left the room.

"What mean h-o-r-m . . . ?" the woman signed. Her face had a contorted, questioning expression.

"Doctor will come back and tell you."

When the doctor returned, he handed her some printed materials about estrogen supplements, which outlined various treatments, their benefits, and possible risks. "Why don't you read these and come back in a few months?" he said.

"I not great read, many big words," she signed.

"I have to see another patient now," he said. "I'll see you next time." He left abruptly. I was stunned. How was this woman to make this important decision about her health without adequate information? I thought about the difference between a Spanish-speaking patient with an interpreter and a deaf one. The Spanish-speaking woman doesn't have to ask her interpreter for explanations. She can ask family members or a Spanish-speaking doctor or read Spanish literature for more information. Where would the deaf woman get this information in a language she could understand? Would it be life threatening if she didn't get it?

Bert was right. Hearing allows us to absorb information that stimulates us intellectually. Without hearing, it's not only difficult to become scholarly, it is difficult to acquire language in the first place. I was reminded of the minimal-language deaf fellow for whom I interpreted in court along with the deaf interpreter who communicated with him through gestures and mime. He was similar to Ildefonso, the deaf adult in Susan Schaller's book, *A Man Without Words*. Ildefonso was an illegal resident from Mexico who had never been to school or exposed to sign language. At twenty-seven-years old, Ildefonso had acquired neither a written, signed, or oral language. Schaller came across Ildefonso in Los Angeles, in a reading class where she was sent to interpret. The first time she signed to him, he could only mimic her movements. Without language, she wrote, "he could not express his thoughts, and he also could not listen—that is, anticipate meaning in others' expressions."[23] No ideas could be exchanged between them other than what they could mime. With mime, they were stuck in the present. The why, when, and where of the action were lost.

Schaller pondered whether Ildefonso understood that he was deaf and different from others because they could hear. How did someone get across the concept of hearing to someone who didn't hear? How it must be for a languageless person to move his lips like he saw others do and not get the same results? Schaller contemplated how it was possible to acquire a sense of morality, of right and wrong, merely by observation.

Riddled with questions, Schaller persisted in trying to communicate with Ildefonso. Eventually, he experienced the same intellectual breakthrough as Helen Keller did at the water pump, and he acquired some sign language skills. Later, Ildefonso led her to a group of deaf adults, all from across the border, who permitted her into their world. She called them languageless, yet she watched them communicating using mime, facial expressions, and gestures. They acted out stories (scenes) in the present tense— how to stay on the U.S. side of the border, how to get work, how to get food. Still, she wondered how they could conceive of a "border" they could not see.

Because language influences our perceptions and understanding, can there really be thoughts without language? Schaller's languageless deaf adults appeared to have thoughts because they had exchanges. Language is what sets humans apart from other animals. Language and communication are required for us to develop into whole human beings, and communication is essential for maintaining our mental and physical health.

•   •   •   •   •

After Bert referred to sign language as a gift of life to an old deaf-blind man, like a mother giving birth to a child, I came across a poem by Erma Bombeck, "Children Are Like Kites." My two teenagers were soon to be out on their own, and raising them had been like trying to fly a kite— not unlike my time with Bert.

He and I had spent months together talking about every aspect of life, learning the fundamentals of sign language, getting off the ground. We practiced and practiced, repeated and repeated. In time, we got up in the air. Sometimes we had setbacks and crashed. But we came back and tried again. We built up our strength and lifted off again. When Bert progressed and needed more string, Jean Kelly and I taught him more sign language. He thirsted for more, reaching out higher and higher. Now sign language was allowing him to sail high in the wind. He was ready to connect with other signers in the world. When he could do that, I would feel I had done my job.

The Big Test

A flyer arrived in the mail announcing a deaf-blind workshop in Colorado Springs to be facilitated by Barb Coffan. It would be similar to the one we attended the year before when Bert was a sign language beginner, but this time there would also be a co-teacher, a deaf and visually impaired man.

Workshops like this didn't come around often. For a long time Bert's wish had been to sign with other deaf people. This could be "The Big Test." Andrea and Vera could join us and take advantage of formal training by deaf-blind experts. The workshop would be important for me, too— to see if I passed the test as Bert's teacher.

I mentioned the workshop to the Riedels. Unfortunately, John and Mary had other plans that weekend. Bert seemed interested yet didn't show a lot of enthusiasm. Nevertheless, even before I knew for sure that we would go, I began talking up the workshop as a motivational tool. "We have to practice your signing so you can talk to the deaf people," I said.

"Yes," Bert agreed, "because the deaf people can't understand me when I talk."

"Let's practice some questions they might ask you. I'll ask you the question and you answer me in sign language. "'What is your name?'"

Bert's habit of dominating the conversation was dramatically altered when he had to sign what he was saying. He replied with labored fingerspelling, "My name is B-e-r-t."

"Where do you live?"

"I live in C-o-n-i-f-e-r," he spelled slowly, making the letter *c* with just two fingers instead of the whole hand.

"What do you like to do?"

"I like to meet people. I like to swim," he signed slowly. "I like to read and *exercise*," he emphasized.

"How old are you?" I queried. Here was incentive for him to practice number signs. They were challenging for beginners, and usually Bert was adept at avoiding them. He preferred counting taps to using signs for numbers.

"How do I say eight-eight?" he asked.

Refreshing his memory, I showed him the sign for the number eight, with the tip of my bent middle finger touching the tip of my thumb. He remembered by himself how to bounce his hand one step to the right to make eighty-eight. Bert had been so used to his old way that he never seemed too eager to work on numbers. Because numbers are involved in nearly all conversations, I was surprised he'd been able to get by for so long using only his tapping and counting method.

Little by little, Bert began showing more enthusiasm about going to the workshop but seemed nervous. I wanted him to feel confident so he'd be successful. "Let's review some signs that pertain to the workshop," I said. We practiced, *deaf, blind, people, talk, sign language,* and even some numbers. We role-played questions for three weeks until he had a list of sentences he could produce in sign language, offering us both a great degree of confidence. I was pleased and proud, ready to show Bert off. We made our decision. We *were* going to the workshop.

• • • • •

On March 18, 2000, I met Andrea and Vera at the Riedels' house at 7 a.m. It was cold and dark outside. Mary was excited yet apprehensive about sending Bert off for the whole day. Bert hadn't been away from his family for any length of time in years. "I feel like a mother sending my kid off to school for the first time," she said. "I have to make sure he has money in his pocket, pack up the braille machine, and put out his warm coat. It's the first time I don't have to worry about someone being home to prepare his lunch!"

It seemed like Christmas morning with all the excitement. John and Mary were still in their pajamas, and Mary was hustling to pack lunch for us. Bert stood in the hall in his polo jacket and baseball cap. He had his cane and his braille copy of the *New York Times* tucked under his arm, waiting to be guided out to the car. He was always ready on time. He had a speech prepared for the class and looked forward to presenting it. Barb had allocated time on the workshop agenda for Bert's presentation.

"I'll take him to the car, Vera, if you can load up the stuff," I suggested. We were all acting like mothers. Andrea and Vera carried the lunch bags and the braille machine while I gingerly walked Bert over the icy driveway to my car. I opened the door to the passenger seat and directed his hand to the opening at the roof so he wouldn't bump his head getting in. He buckled his seatbelt. Andrea and Vera piled into the backseat. Like kids in a yellow school bus, we blew kisses, waved good-byes, and shook the "I love you" sign to John and Mary. The dust twirled behind us as we pulled up the dirt road.

"Hey, Bert, we're going to Colorado Springs," I announced. He didn't hear me. He had his braille newspaper on his lap, prepared for a long drive. Mary had made a new rule. We were not allowed to engage in sign conversation while driving. There'd been too many close calls trying to answer Bert's questions with one hand while driving with the other. I felt guilty for ignoring him for our two-hour trip, but we needed to respect Mary's viewpoint. Instead, the three of us girls passed the time quickly with our chatter.

As we neared Colorado Springs, I saw the sparkling spires atop the Air Force Academy chapel, tucked into the foothills, and soon our exit number. "Here's our exit," I said. "At least I think it is. Bert's sitting on the paper with the directions." I remembered laying them on his seat before we got into the car.

"Good one, Diane! Who's going to reach under there to get them?" Andrea asked.

Laughing, I said, "I think the college is just off the highway."

Andrea spotted the sign before I did. "There . . . Pikes Peak Community College. Rampart Range Campus."

We took the exit to a road leading eastward, which seemed opposite of what I'd been told. We went a mile further and stopped at a red light. Andrea buzzed her window down, calling out for directions to a man in a pickup in the next lane. Leaning out his window, he quickly called them back as the light changed. "Turn left here, and follow the road around the curve. It's a brown building on the right."

I glanced at my watch as we drove into the parking lot. It was 8:45 a.m. We were going to arrive on time. Bert felt the car stop. "Are we here?" he asked, relieved he could talk at last.

Andrea reached over from the backseat. "Yes," she answered, with two taps on his shoulder. We all happily disembarked out into an icy cold wind. Andrea met Bert as he hoisted himself out of the car and led him toward the building. Vera and I loaded the lunch bags and backpacks over our shoulders and started up the sidewalk after them.

Inside the building, I looked around for signs pointing the way to the deaf-blind workshop. There were no signs. I led Bert to the washroom and waited in the hall while Vera walked off in search of the classroom. She came back shrugging her shoulders with a maintenance man close behind.

"He doesn't know where the deaf-blind workshop is," Vera said.

"I don't believe there is a workshop here," the man said with a puzzled expression. He left to check the building's activity schedule. Andrea retrieved Bert from the washroom. The maintenance man returned. "Nope, there's no workshop here today," he said. A security guard had joined us by then. Bert was standing patiently quiet, without knowing what was going on.

"This is Pikes Peak Community College isn't it?" I asked.

"Yes, Rampart Range Campus," the security guard answered.

"You mean there's another campus in this town?"

He nodded. "The other one's on the south part of town, at Exit 135." It was ten minutes past the start time of the workshop. Bert didn't even know we were at the wrong place. Vera and I ran toward the parking lot with the lunch bags bumping against our backsides. Andrea spelled to Bert, "*w-r-o-n-g*" and led him hurriedly toward the door.

"Wrong building," he chuckled, shuffling along.

My Type A personality kicked in. I hated being late. Now we'd have to make a big entrance with our entourage. Our arrival would interrupt the workshop. We still had to get the braille machine set up, do our greetings, and get Bert situated. Barb had hired a translator for Bert who needed to be oriented on how to use the machine. All eyes would be on us. This was not what I had planned. This was supposed to have been a special and perfect day.

With the car repacked, we pulled out of the parking lot. I drove faster this time.

"Hold on everyone, we're gonna get there." We swayed with the car careening around the curve. The exit we needed was fifteen more miles down the highway. The paper with the directions I thought Bert was sitting on was nowhere to be found. We'd have to trust the security guard's instructions.

At 9:30 a.m. we saw the sign for Pikes Peak Community College, Centennial Campus. In all the hurried confusion we hadn't explained to Bert what was happening. We couldn't communicate in the car either, speeding down the highway. He gathered for himself we had gotten lost. He was going with the flow.

The college was just off the highway to the west. I dropped the three of them off to save time. I had all the bags with me. The last parking space available was down a hill at the far end of the long building.

My hair blew across my face in the biting cold when I stepped from the car. I gathered the three bags and my video camera from the back of the station wagon, hoisting two of them over each shoulder. It was hard to walk fast, uphill against the strong wind. "What am I doing?" I muttered. "I've just had surgery. Why am I trying to carry all this stuff?" Out of shape, I pushed toward the nearest door breathing hard. It was locked. I walked around the building to the next one. Every step felt like extreme slow motion. My heart beat hard and fast. Luckily the door was unlocked. I started down the long hall with no idea where

I was going. The bags were heavy and cut into my shoulders. I was panting, dredging up the last bit of my energy.

Andrea's voice carried from around a corner. I thought surely she'd found a sign pointing the way to the classroom. When we met up in the lobby, confused and frustrated, each of us talked fast. Bert was quietly confused, as we passed him from one of us to the other.

"Did you find it?" I asked. They both shook their heads. The building was huge and oddly shaped. Classrooms lined both sides of long hallways going every which way. There were three floors with hundreds of classrooms and walkways connecting to other buildings housing machine shops and auto body shops. Vera headed in one direction and Andrea in another, looking for some clue that would lead us to the workshop. I stayed with Bert and tried to catch my breath.

"We can't f-i-n-d class," I signed quickly in his hand.

"Camp?" Bert couldn't read my signs that fast. He sensed my impatience.

"No. We c-a-n-t," I spelled. "We forgot something."

He still didn't understand me. I was totally frustrated. I spelled Vera's name and gestured that she had gone somewhere to the left and Andrea was scouting to the right.

"Oh, they're looking all over," he said.

Vera returned. "Nothing," she reported, out of breath. I feared we'd come all this way with high hopes, only to be disappointed. We were going to miss the workshop because I didn't have the room number. Andrea came back out of breath, too, with the librarian. They'd been looking through catalogs for the class. The librarian knew nothing about a deaf-blind workshop.

As we stood in front of an elevator door, suddenly I thought of Mary. "Maybe she has a copy of the flyer I faxed her. The room number should be on it." We set our bags down and I pulled a cell phone from my backpack, hoping she was home. When the elevator door opened, a man stepped out and tripped over our bags. All of us were embarrassed. Vera helped him up.

There was no answer at the Riedels.

"Try her cell," Vera offered, giving me the number.

This time Mary answered. Conscious of precious minutes passing, I dispensed with the usual polite greeting. "Mary, we can't find the room. This building is huge. Do you still have the flyer with a room number on it?"

It seemed like a long wait while Mary searched for the flyer. I was figuring out what we would do next if this didn't work. I felt like Nancy Drew trying to solve a mystery. Mary came back with good news. "Room A169."

I clapped into Bert's hands. "Yea! We know—"

"Ohhhh, you got it now." He read my body language.

Andrea spun around looking for a map of the building in the lobby. "Now where the heck is room A169?" Together this time, we marched off down the long hall, laden with the backpacks. Bert held tightly onto my arm trying to keep up with my quickening steps. We reached an exit door at the end of the hall. There was no room A169 down that hall. It was 10:05 and we were still lost. Vera ran ahead. A school employee directed her outside across a courtyard to another door. Andrea and I waited with Bert, watching her to see if the door was unlocked before dragging Bert out into the cold wind.

We moved swiftly after Vera when we saw her open the door. When my hair blew across my face once more, I was muttering again, "I can't believe this." Bert was still not complaining. And Andrea, she was a continuous out-loud thinker. She was irritated and muttering, too, as we trudged across the courtyard.

Vera appeared in a second-floor window overlooking us down below. She motioned something I couldn't understand. Had she known sign language, we could have communicated through the window. Instead, she ran back down the stairs to meet us at the door. She'd found the room.

Barb had been worried when we hadn't shown up early but started the workshop punctually, trusting we'd eventually arrive. She introduced Bert and me in our absence. Bert was an important part of her daylong seminar. She told the participants that when we did arrive, she'd suspend everything, knowing that a deaf-blind person doesn't slide easily into a class in progress.

Pushing my embarrassment aside, I apologized to the class for our tardiness. Barb made the awkwardness easier by calling a refreshment break, which allowed us

Bert speaking at the deaf-blind workshop in Colorado Springs.

Barb Coffan talks with Bert while Andrea Duykers, Vera Feistal, and I embrace the moment.

time to make the transition. Andrea efficiently set up Bert's machine in record speed and oriented the waiting translator on how to use it. I watched Bert adapt readily to the circumstances. He sat down and began to read his brailler. At last he had access to fluid communication. I drew in some deep breaths, assured now that we would accomplish what we set out to do.

Barb resumed her lecture about the causes of deafblindness and reviewed the various modes of communication used. Bert was able to follow her lecture on his braille machine as the translator entered the words into the computer. I felt content knowing he was no longer being left out of the interaction and that Vera and Andrea were free to concentrate on the lecture. This was what we had come for. The real test, however, was still ahead.

No More Pretending

When I first came into Bert's life, I wondered whether it was even possible for him to learn sign language. After it became clear that he was capable of learning far more than what Mary initially envisioned as a few "basic signs," my dream became for him to be able to communicate with any signer. Not only would this open up Bert's world, it was essential for his safety. I knew if I had his family's support, we could get there.

Ten months after starting our lessons, we attended Barb Coffan's first deaf-blind workshop. Bert was a tenderfoot then. He wasn't able to converse with strangers using sign language, and when Shana, the teacher of deaf-blind children in Illinois, returned to visit him during those early months of lessons, he didn't understand her signs. The Riedels were disappointed. "That was to be expected," Shana explained. "There are variations of sign language. It takes time to learn them."

Bert had come a long way since then, considering his age and numerous obstacles. Now he stood in front of twenty-eight interpreters and sign language students, delivering his "Midas Touch" speech. I sat to his left, ready to lend support should he feel lost at any point, talking to an audience he could only imagine. He spoke confidently, securely stationed behind the lectern. He didn't reach out to me once during his speech.

The class listened raptly to Bert's story and when he finished they asked him questions. I stood next to him for this part so I could interpret. Fortunately, some of the questions were ones we had rehearsed, so he read my signs with relative ease. I was relieved he didn't get flustered, and he only tripped up once—on the sign for *girl,* when someone asked if he was looking for a girlfriend.

In the next part of the training, we paired up to practice techniques Barb had taught us for guiding deaf-blind persons: going up and down stairs, over curbs, through narrow spaces, into restrooms, drinking at water fountains, or investigating tactilely interesting objects. One person in each pair wore a blindfold and earplugs to simulate deaf-blindness while the other person acted as a guide. The pairs set off walking down hallways to explore the building. Vera was paired with Diane Anderson, the deaf wife of our co-teacher. Bert was paired with Linda Worman, a sign language student.

Linda introduced herself to Bert through the translator on the brailler and told him she would be his guide. "Hello, Linda," he said. "How long have you been studying sign language?" She held two fingers up to his hand.

"Two years?"

"Yes," she said with two taps. Barb had informed the class about the method Bert used for *yes* and *no.*

"How old are you?" he asked.

Barb interrupted them before Linda got a chance to answer his question. Barb let them know they needed to get going on their walk. Jovially, Bert unfolded his cane and, as the good sport he always was, pushed himself up with an "umph" and trotted off with Linda, singing.

With my video camera up to my eye, I accompanied them down the hall. I noticed Bert took to her "soft spoken" manner immediately. It came across in her gentle signing. She reminded me of his daughter Marcia.

Linda stopped them in front of the elevator and spelled a little nervously, "*e-l—*"

"Elevator, sure," Bert said. "It's up to you."

She made an upward motion with her hand over her other arm. "Okay, we're going up," he said. On the second floor they passed blindfolded Vera, coupled with Diane Anderson. Vera was running her hands over the opening to a pop machine.

"I have question," Linda signed.

"Have what?"

"Q-u-e-s—"

"Was that a *p* or a *q*?"

"*Q*."

"Question. Let me show you how to sign that," Bert said self-assuredly. He outlined the question mark in the air with his index finger, just as I had taught him.

"Are you tired?" she asked him.

"Oh, noooo. I love to walk," Bert replied. He was never tired.

Blindfolded, Andrea passed us with her guide. She held onto the guide's arm with one hand and trailed the wall with her fingertips of her other. None of the pairs in the hallways were speaking, only signing and feeling things, except Bert, who was chattering nonstop.

"H-a-l-l, color, white, b-o-r-i-n-g," Linda signed.

"Hall, boring? What do you mean? What's a boring room?" Bert wondered.

"Color, boring." Linda repeated.

"Is that a color, 'boring'?"

"White is boring," she signed.

"White's not really a color," Bert said. "Black isn't either.

It's just the absence of color. It reminds me of March sixteenth, the day after a Colorado snowstorm. My daughter-in-law, Mary, described it to me this way:

Today the world is bathed in pureness.
Fluffy, falling snow.
Glistening as sparkling diamonds, graced
   by the sun.
The forest and the mountains also wear
the cloak of purity.
Here's a mighty sight that makes the soul soar.

"It's all about white. It's really very beautiful," he said.

Linda smiled and tapped him twice. With my video camera rolling, I followed Bert and Linda back to the classroom. She needed to switch partners to practice with the blindfold. Diane Anderson joined Bert in the classroom while most of the other pairs were still exploring the hallways.

"Me, deaf," Diane signed in Bert's hand.

This came out of the blue to Bert. He misread her. "Your daughter?"

"Me, deaf, me," she repeated.

A professional interpreter in solid-colored dress stood behind Bert, signing his words. Diane picked up from the interpreter what she couldn't read from Bert's lips. Diane signed her name to Bert. "Me, D-i-a-n-e."

"Is this Diane, my sign language teacher? How are you, sweetheart? No, this must be another Diane. Are you the one with the long hair?" He reached out to feel her hair and then answered himself, "No, that's another Diane."

"Me deaf," she explained.

"You're deaf. For heaven's sake. Tell me more about yourself." Suddenly, Bert remembered he needed to sign to deaf people. He started over, slowly signing this time. "Tell, me, more, about, you."

"Me, baby, born deaf."

"Wait, do it again."

"B-o-r-n," she spelled.

"I see. Where were you born?"

"I born deaf."

"That's not the sign for Colorado," Bert thought out loud. "Oh, you were born deaf. That's a tough life." Diane nodded her head along with her sign *yes.* Bert wanted to know where Diane Anderson lived. Were her parents deaf? Was her life hard? What was the cause of her deafness, and what did she like to do? All of us who were watching broke out in surprised laughter when she said she liked to play the piano. Bert got excited about that. He asked her if she played Beethoven's "Minuet in G." "Do you remember it? It goes like this: "'Da-da Da-da Da-da Da-da Daaaa,'" he sang. "Or maybe you remember the rhythm?"

Diane Anderson was laughing and enjoying Bert without any idea how special this moment was for me. I was elated. My dream, and his wish, had come true. Bert was communicating in sign language with a Deaf person.

• • • • •

On the drive home from Colorado Springs I became hoarse from laughing so much. "This day was unbelievable. The morning felt like one of those bad dreams where you just can't get to where you're trying to be," I said.

"Yeah, but at least we weren't naked!" Vera said. All our tension from the morning released into gales of laughter. Bert sat quietly through our celebration. We were keenly aware that, in spite of his progress, he still wasn't able to share in the moment every time.

At Bert's house I led him up the steps to the front door. Vera and Andrea drove away as Bert and I stepped into the entryway. He shared what he was thinking. "I'm moving forward now. I went through eighty years of my life, fighting and pretending. Sign language has brought me back. I can never give it up, even if I never write another article. I'm a happy man . . . I feel normal. I don't have to pretend anymore."

His words drew me back to the poem about the kite. Ours was flying high and steady. Sign language was a part of him now, and I knew Bert could make it on his own. He could soar as he was meant to soar.

Feeling euphoric, I watched Bert hang his jacket in the closet and with a tight hug we said good-bye. All was quiet in the house then, except for the soft tap-tapping of his cane across the floor as he headed toward his piano.

Epilogue

Halfway into Bert's ninety-second year, we were still enjoying our sign language lessons in spite of days when Bert mixed up day with night or confused dreams with reality. We made every hour count. One day he expressed that he might not have much time left on this earth, and he decided he wanted a party. He invited his friends and everyone at the Life Care Center to an ice-cream social on the Fourth of July. He wanted dancing, so Andrea found an old phonograph and brought all the old standards Bert loved. Wearing a white suit complete with a red rose pinned to his lapel, Bert asked that I spell each woman's name into his hand so he would know who he was dancing with. With each dance he smiled brighter. Four months later, after a brief illness, Bert died peacefully on November 25, 2003.

Notes

PROLOGUE

1. Elizabeth Gold, "Signing Your Mind," *Coloradan* (University of Colorado alumni magazine), May 2001.

CHAPTER 1

2. Boys Town National Research Hospital, National Center for the Study and Treatment of Usher Syndrome, www.boystownhospital.org/ UsherSyndrome/index.asp, accessed February 2004.

CHAPTER 2

3. McCay Vernon, "Looking Back Looking Forward: A Half-Century of Progress for Deaf Individuals," *CSD Spectrum* (Summer 2002): 12–15.

4. Christine Yoshinaga-Itano et al., "Language of Early- and Later-Identified Children with Hearing Loss," *Pediatrics* 102, no. 5 (November 1998): 1161.

5. Elizabeth Gold, "Signing Your Mind," *Coloradan* (University of Colorado alumni magazine), May 2001.

CHAPTER 3

6. Laura Bridgman was thirty-six years older than Anne Sullivan. "After Sullivan learned the manual alphabet—probably from Laura herself—the two spent many hours talking." Elisabeth Gitter, *The Imprisoned Guest* (New York: Farrar, Straus, and Giroux, 2001), 280.

7. Helen Keller, *The Story of My Life* (Cutchogue, N.Y.: Buccaneer Books, 1976), 266.

8. Ibid., 325.

CHAPTER 4

9. Leah Hager Cohen, *Train Go Sorry* (New York: Houghton Mifflin Company, 1994), 116.

10. Fortunately for deaf students today, the inadequacies of deaf education of the past—poorly trained teachers and unskilled interpreters—have been acknowledged and steps have been made to rectify the situation. Interpreter training programs sprang up throughout the country beginning in the mid-1970s. In the 1990s, states began establishing standards for interpreters. In 1996, a distance learning program called Educational Interpreting Certificate Program was established to better prepare interpreters

who work in the schools. It includes a variety of technologies and online instruction. Colorado passed a law in 1997 mandating that interpreters who work in the public schools pass an assessment demonstrating minimum standards of proficiency. In 1999 and 2000, four other states passed laws requiring interpreters to be licensed or certified.

CHAPTER 5

11. Mark Ross, "Speechreading," www.therubins.com/geninfo/speechrd.htm; grant from the National Institute on Disability and Rehabilitation Research to the Lexington Center, Jackson Heights, N.Y., September 1999.

12. Gabriel Grayson, *Talking with Your Hands, Listening with Your Eye: A Complete Photographic Guide to American Sign Language* (Garden City Park, N.Y.: Square One Publishers, 2003).

CHAPTER 8

13. Bert Riedel, "One Deaf-Blind Man's Dream," *Nat-Cent News* (the newsletter for the National Helen Keller Institute, Sands Point, New York) 29, no.1 (September 1998): 37.

CHAPTER 12

14. McCay Vernon and Katrina Miller, "Characteristics of the Sign Languages of the Deaf in Relationship to Interpreting," *Journal of Interpretation* (a publication of the Registry of Interpreters for the Deaf, Inc.) (2001): 103.

CHAPTER 20

15. I was unable to verify the existence of the "Chicago School for the Blind"; it is likely that Bert actually attended the Illinois Industrial Home for the Blind, which appears in the *1951 Social Service Directory,* published by the Welfare Council of Metropolitan Chicago. See also State Department of Correctional Service, *Services for the Blind: Manual of Administrative Procedures,* May 1, 1954.

CHAPTER 26

16. Oliver Sacks, *An Anthropologist on Mars* (New York: Alfred A. Knopf, 1995), 119.

17. Alberto Valvo, *Sight Restoration After Long-Term Blindness: The Problems and Behavior Patterns of Visual Rehabilitation* (New York: American Foundation for the Blind, 1971), 9.

18. Ibid., 29.

19. Braille readers have an enlarged area of cerebral cortex where information perceived through the reading finger is processed. The area of the brain normally used to interpret visual information becomes allocated for touch in the blind. Researchers have captured this phenomenon using positron emission tomography (PET). In blind persons, the PET shows increased blood flow to the visual cortical areas. See Roy H. Hamilton and Alvaro Pascual-Leone, "Cortical Plasticity Associated with Braille Learning," *Trends in Cognitive Sciences* 2, no. 5 (May 1998). Similarly, in deaf persons the auditory part of the brain designated for speech becomes allocated for visual language. In deaf persons who use sign language, there is increased blood flow to the auditory cortical areas, indicating the brain's marvelous ability to reorganize and adapt. See Daniel McCabe, "New Light on Language," *McGill-Reporter,* November 6, 1997, McGill University, Montreal, Quebec, Canada.

CHAPTER 27

20. Arden Neisser, *The Other Side of Silence* (New York: Alfred A. Knopf, 1983), 24.

21. Don Renzulli, "A Tribute to Louie J. Fant, Jr.," *VIEWS* (a monthly publication of the Registry of Interpreters for the Deaf) 18, no. 7 (July 2001).

22. Louie Fant, "Drama and Poetry in Sign Language: A Personal Reminiscence," *Sign Language and the Deaf Community* (Silver Spring, Md.: National Association of the Deaf, 1980), 199.

CHAPTER 33

23. Susan Schaller, *A Man Without Words* (New York: Summit Books, 1991), 108.

Bibliography

Abrams, Charlotte. *The Silents.* Washington, D.C.: Gallaudet University Press, 1996.

American Academy of Pediatrics. "Joint Committee on Infant Hearing: 1994 Position Statement." *Pediatrics* 95, no. 1 (1994): 152–156.

Bailey, Kimberly. "Mental Health Issues in the Deaf Community." About.com, Inc., 2001.

Baker, Charlotte, and Robbin Battison. *Sign Language and the Deaf Community: Essays in Honor of William Stokoe.* Silver Spring, Md.: National Association of the Deaf, 1980.

Baker-Shenk, Charlotte, and Dennis Cokely. *American Sign Language: A Teacher's Resource Text on Grammar and Culture.* Washington, D.C.: Gallaudet University Press, 1991. First published 1980 by T.J. Publishers, Inc.

Bombeck, Erma. "Children Are Like Kites." *Forever, Erma.* Kansas City, Mo.: Andrews and McMeel, 1996.

Boyle, Maureen. "Deaf Suspect's Case a Problem for Court." *Standard Times,* October 11, 1996.

Bransford, John D., Ann L. Brown, and Rodney R. Cocking, eds. "Mind and Brain." In *How People Learn: Brain, Mind, Experience, and School.* http://www.nap.edu/html/howpeople1/ch5.html.

Cohen, Leah Hager. *Train Go Sorry.* Boston: Houghton Mifflin Company, 1994.

Davis, Lennard J. "Prisoners of Silence." *The Nation,* October 4, 1993.

Friedman, Alan, James Webb, and Richard Lewak. *Psychological Assessment with the MMPI.* Hillsdale, N.J.: Lawrence Erlbaum Associates, 1989.

Gitter, Elisabeth. *The Imprisoned Guest.* New York: Farrar, Straus, and Giroux, 2001.

Gold, Elizabeth. "Signing Your Mind." *Coloradan* (University of Colorado alumni magazine), May 2001.

Grayson, Gabriel. *Talking with Your Hands, Listening with Your Eyes: A Complete Photographic Guide to American Sign Language.* Garden City Park, N.Y.: Square One Publishers, 2003.

Greenberg, Joanne. *Of Such Small Differences.* New York: Holt, Rinehart, and Winston, 1988.

Hine, Robert V. *Second Sight,* Berkeley: University of California Press, 1993.

Keller, Helen. *The Story of My Life.* Cutchogue, N.Y.: Buccaneer Books, 1976.

Jacobs, Leo. *A Deaf Adult Speaks Out.* Washington, D.C.: Gallaudet College Press, 1969.

Laborit, Emmanuelle. *Cry of the Gull.* Washington, D.C.: Gallaudet University Press, 1998.

Marshark, Marc. *Raising and Educating a Deaf Child.* New York: Oxford University Press On Demand, 1998.

McCabe, Daniel. "New Light on Language." *McGill-Reporter,* November 6, 1997.

McGill University. "McGill Researchers Present Major Findings at US Neurosciences Conference." News release. Montreal, Quebec, Canada. October 28, 1997.

Medical Economics Company. "What If Your Patient Is Also Deaf?" Copyright 1976 by Litton Industries, Inc. Reprinted in *RN Magazine,* June 1976.

Mindel, Eugene, and McCay Vernon. *They Grow in Silence.* Silver Spring, Md.: National Association of the Deaf, 1971.

Moore, Timothy. "Competence to Stand Trial." *Gale Encyclopedia of Psychology.* 2nd ed. Farmington Hills, Mich.: Gale Group, 2001.

Neisser, Arden. *The Other Side of Silence.* New York: Alfred A. Knopf, 1983.

Nieminen, Raija. *Voyage to the Island.* Washington, D.C.: Gallaudet University Press, 1990.

Owens, Pam. *Handbook for Interpreters in the Mental Health Setting.* Overland Park, Kans:. Johnson County Community College, n.d.

Pollard, Robert. "Psychological Testing and Assessment." Chapter for a training manual by the Institute on Deafness, Department of Communicative Disorders, Northern Illinois University.

Porter, Anne. "Sign Language Interpretation in Psychotherapy with Deaf Patients." *American Journal of Psychotherapy* 53, no. 2 (Spring 1999).

Renzulli, Don. "A Tribute to Louie J. Fant, Jr." *VIEWS* (a monthly publication of the Registry of Interpreters for the Deaf) 18, no. 7 (July 2001).

Riedel, Bert. "One Deaf-Blind Man's Dream." *Nat-Cent News* (newsletter for the National Helen Keller Institute, Sands Point, N.Y.) 29, no. 1 (September 1998): 37.

Ross, Mark. "Speechreading." Grant #RH133E30015 from the U.S. Department of Education, NIDRR, to the Lexington Center, Jackson Heights, N.Y., 1999.

Sacks, Oliver. *An Anthropologist On Mars.* New York: Knopf, 1995.

Schaller, Susan. *A Man Without Words.* New York: Simon and Schuster, 1991.

Smith, Theresa. *Guidelines: Practical Tips for Working and Socializing with Deaf-Blind People.* Burtonsville, Md.: Sign Media, Inc., 1994.

Smith, Theresa. *Guidelines for Working/Playing with Deaf-Blind People.* Paper, 1997.

Smithdas, Robert J. *Life at My Fingertips.* Garden City, N.Y.: Doubleday, 1958.

Smithdas, Robert J. *Shared Beauty.* New York: Portal Press, 1982.

Stansfield, Millie. "Psychological Issues in Mental Health Interpreting." *RID Interpreting Journal* 1, no. 1 (1981): 18–31.

State Department of Correctional Service. *Services for the Blind: Manual of Administrative Procedures.* May 1, 1954.

Steinberg, Annie G., Vicki Joy Sullivan, and Ruth C. Loew. "Cultural and Linguistic Barriers to Mental Health Service Access: The Deaf Consumer's Perspective." *American Journal of Psychiatry* 155, no. 7 (July 1998): 982–984.

Valvo, Alberto. *Sight Restoration After Long-Term Blindness: The Problems and Behavior Patterns of Visual Rehabilitation.* New York: American Foundation for the Blind, 1971.

Vernon, McCay. "Looking Back Looking Forward: A Half-Century of Progress for Deaf Individuals." *CSD Spectrum* (Summer 2002): 12–15.

Vernon, McCay, and Katrina Miller. "Characteristics of the Sign Languages of the Deaf in Relationship to Interpreting." *Journal of Interpretation* (a publication of the Registry of Interpreters for the Deaf, Inc.) (2001): 103.

Walker, Lou Ann. *A Loss for Words.* New York: Harper and Row, 1986.

Walker, Lou Ann. "They're Breaking the Sound Barrier." *Parade Magazine,* May 13, 2001.

Yoshinaga-Itano, Christine et al. "Language of Early- and Later-Identified Children with Hearing Loss." *Pediatrics* 102, no. 5 (November 1998): 1161.

About the Author

DIANE CHAMBERS, a native of Colorado and graduate of the University of Colorado in Boulder, has worked as a professional sign language interpreter for twenty-seven years. Diane lives with her husband on Conifer Mountain, in Colorado, where they raised their two children. She is working on her next book, *Hearing the Stream,* about breast cancer.

To order Words in My Hands

from Ellexa Press, LLC, go to:

www.ellexapress@CityMax.com

Fax (303) 838-7010

Or send check or money order with this form to:
Ellexa Press, LLC
32262 Steven Way
Conifer, CO 80433

$15.95 per copy

Number of copies _____ x $15.95 = _____

Shipping and handling $4 per 1–2 copies = _____

CO residents add 4.2% sales tax = _____

Total = _____

Name _____

Address _____

_____

City/State _____

Zip _____ **Phone** _____

Fax _____ **Email** _____

Payment by credit card
☐ VISA ☐ MasterCard

Card number _____

Name on card _____

Expiration date _____